POETRY on RECORD

98 POETS READ THEIR WORK

1888~2006

Producer's Note
Rebekah Presson Mosby
- 3 -

A Quiet Shout
Al Young
- 5 -

Our Lives Distilled
Rebekah Presson Mosby
- 15 -

Track List & Poet Biographies
Rebekah Presson Mosby
- 39 -

so much depends
upon

a red wheel
barrow

"The Red Wheelbarrow" by William Carlos Williams

glazed with rain
water

beside the white
chickens.

Producer's Note

Poetry On Record: 98 Poets Read Their Work (1888-2006) is not intended as a canonical work of the greatest-ever poems written by the greatest poets. Rather, it tells a sort of story about the past century and a half of poetry in English, from Romanticism to Modernism, from the Harlem Renaissance to Black Arts to hip-hop, from rhyme and meter to free verse, from Confessionalism to New Formalism, from lyric to narrative to epic and back until it reaches Jonathan Lamfers, a recent college graduate whose "scab" follows the historical tradition of Whitman and Ginsberg and reflects the numbness and insecurity felt by many young people coming up after 9/11.

Poetry On Record is more comprehensive than any similar collection preceding it, including those I shaped (*In Their Own Voices: A Century Of Recorded Poetry, Our Souls Have Grown Deep Like The Rivers: Black Poets Read Their Work* and, as co-editor with Elise Paschen, *Poetry Speaks*). All the same, not all the great poets are here. The frustrations of trying to fit the entire history of recorded poetry onto a four-CD set were many, and I deeply regret the fine, mostly living poets whose words are not included here. A list of names would be too long to feature; suffice it to say that it is simply the case that the early and mid-20th century produced an extraordinary number of excellent poets.

Listening to this collection, you will not only be able to trace trends and movements in English language poetry over the past century and a half or so, but you will also hear how the style of reading poetry has changed, how technology has influenced the way poetry is performed and, of course, how new technologies have changed the sound of the recorded voice. Most importantly, you will hear wonderful poems read by their authors in the way the authors want them to be read.

— *Rebekah Presson Mosby*
Paris, October 2005

A QUIET SHOUT

by AL YOUNG

When in 2005 Governor Arnold Schwarzenegger appointed me Poet Laureate of California, I had no idea what my responsibilities would entail.

"Why would you even want this job?" the Governor asked, igniting his cigar. The interview took place in the plush office-tent he'd had set up on Sacramento's capitol grounds, where it was OK to smoke. "It pays no money, and you're going to be busy."

"I welcome the chance," I said, "to give something back to a state that has given me so much."

"And, as a poet, are you political?"

"Very political," I said, "and I intend to get even more political."

"Why?" he wanted to know.

"Because, Governor, these are dark times."

I looked back at his four advisors for this appointment, all of them women, who sat behind me, facing the gubernatorial desk.

"You do understand that you will be expected to be present at six official venues during your two-year appointment. And you must declare a major project. What is your special project?"

"I would like to develop a Web site to give California's poets and students and fans of poetry access to poetry texts, audio and video recordings of readings and other poetry events, as well as Webcasts, lectures and discussions. Susan Hildreth, the State Librarian, loves the idea and says she looks forward to working with me."

"Very good," he said with a smile, peeping at the notes on his well-polished desk. "Now, back to politics. In this poem of yours called 'Conjugal Visits,' you say — and here Governor Schwarzenegger recited by heart:

'All these Black men crammed up in jail,
all this I.Q. on ice,
while governments, bank presidents,
the Mafia don't think twice.

They fly in dope and make real sure
they hands stay nice and clean.
The chump-change Reece made on the street
— what's that supposed to mean?'

We real cool

by Gwendolyn Brooks

The pool players.
7 at the Golden Shovel.

We real cool. We
Left school. We

Lurk late. We
Strike straight. We

Sing sin. We
Thin gin. We

Jazz June. We
Die soon.

More than taken aback that he had taken time to zero in on and memorize a passage of a particular poem of mine, I said, "Well, Governor, you surprise me."

"Yes," he said with a disarming grin. "You would not think I would like a poem like this, where you're saying such things about the government. But I like it. I do. You know why?"

From a lifetime of watching the ways in which poetry, music and all the other arts continue to leap the tallest walls and ease across the tightest of borders, I sat prepared for yet another surprise.

"First of all," the Governor said, "I follow hip-hop. Secondly, I, too, am for prison reform."

Energized by the tension the advisors behind me transmitted, I said, "You write a poem, you express something, but you never really know how a reader or listener will take it."

"As a fellow artist, Mr. Young, I know this well. In *Terminator* there is a scene, where I go into an L.A. police precinct and mow down several people — blam-blam-blam! — just like that. Well, my fans in the hip-hop community tell me: 'Oh, Arnold, that is such a cool scene!' But my fans in the L.A.P.D. community — they like it too. So you go figure."

I left the tent, certain the Governor would surely select one of the other four contenders, someone "safe" — if any poet or any poem is ever truly "safe." But days later, while on a train up to Washington state to give a jazz-and-poetry fundraiser reading for *The Seattle Review*, I got a call from National Public Radio. Responding to a press release I hadn't yet seen, they wanted to break the news of the appointment by having me read my poem "To Be The Perfect Fool."

The perfect fool. It isn't unusual for courses of instruction to bear such titles as Chemistry for Poets, Calculus for Poets, Auto Repair for Poets or Government for Poets. Even now in this new century the idea of a poet as someone dislocated from the real world and real time persists. Meanwhile, in the heart of this very darkness, the lessons our species clearly has not learned from the previous century flutter in tatters on warmed global breezes. In the 20th century we slaughtered more than 100 million of our own kind: *Homo sapiens*. "Wise man" is still the English translation of this Latin word.

Inevitably poetry surfaces when times get bad. I saw it happen during my own formative years, which happened to coincide with the McCarthy Era in America. The unprecedented popularity of Welsh bard Dylan Thomas' four U.S. reading tours during the 1950s may have signaled the poetry explosion that lay ahead. It was during that sullen, repressive decade — when we took it for granted that the world would probably go up in a nuclear cloudburst — that Beat Generation and the Black Mountain poets and novelists captured the nation's literary stage. Allen Ginsberg, Gregory Corso, Gary Snyder, Diane di Prima, LeRoi Jones (aka Amiri Baraka), William Burroughs, Lawrence Ferlinghetti, Ted Joans, novelists Jack Kerouac and John Clellon Holmes, Robert Creeley, Denise Levertov, Charles Olson — many of these anti-establishment writers challenged institutionalized power and hypocrisy.

As Harry Belafonte tells it, Red Channels was the name of the renowned directory that TV host Ed Sullivan consulted when he wanted to find out if it were permissible to have the gifted performer on *Toast Of The Town*. As one of the few channels that never gets blocked — that remains unmediated — poetry matters. You can have your say in poetry, which will always remain a populist medium. Poetry belongs to everyone and to no one. Don't tell my professor friends I said so — not unless you would also have them remember that Plato excluded poets from his Republic on the basis that they don't tell the truth.

"The telling of truth is the poet's proper domain," I state in a musical memoir called *Body And Soul: Coleman Hawkins, 1939*, "and in the head-whipping nations of this darkening, fact-ridden world, people still look to poets and music they make for light, sweet light illumining everything everywhere." As a poet laureate, I know it's going to take more than status and charm to either remind my sisters and brothers or make them

"Ray"
(excerpt)
by Hayden Carruth

What crazies we writers are our heads full of language like buckets of minnows standing in the moonlight on a dock. Ray was a good writer, a wonderful writer, and his poems are good, most of them and they made me cry, there at my kitchen table with my head down, me, a sixty-seven-year-old galoot, an old fool because all old men are fools, they have to be, shoveling big jagged chunks of that ordinary pie into my mouth, and the water falling from my eyes onto the pie, the plate, my hand, little speckles shining in the light, brightening the colors, and I ate that goddamn pie, and it tasted good to me.

remember why civilizations, nations, states, regions are remembered for their culture. "If Britain hadn't produced anything else," one Londoner informed me, "William Shakespeare would've been quite enough. That alone would've given us all the power, all the basic clout we needed."

If poetry isn't basic, then what is? If the DNA of the world doesn't turn out not to be poetry, then what? If at the heart of every bone and stone and ruin and moan you don't come face to face with poetry, have you been wasting your life?

What else except poetry could possibly lie beneath all façades, all masks, all surfaces and appearances? My Silicon Valley computer guru Ed Bigelow once told me: "When I write what turns out to be an elegant program, to me it's like writing poetry." When a mathematician creates a wildly beautiful equation, what shines and pulsates at the other side of that equal sign, that bottom-line sum-up is poetry. Where I might compose a sonnet, she cooks up a broth in math. Thus do we signal and wave and touch and speak to each other.

"Talking with one another is loving one another," so the ancient Kenyan proverb goes. Just as speakers and listeners collude and comply, so readers and writers form one conjugal unit. I have come to believe that the most moving and meaningful poetry occurs in private, while poets, playwrights, novelists, songwriters, screenwriters and other storytellers slip us an awful lot of lovely, moving lines in their portrayals of everyday people whose lives have been derailed or in some way set off-course by war, by death, sickness, by loss, by betrayal, by sudden good fortune or by love.

"How many of y'all still believe in love?" a stand-up comic played by Martin Lawrence asks of his comedy club audience in the movie *Talkin' Dirty After Dark*. By the time he asks onscreen for a show of hands, imagination, puffing on me, has exhaled me out to graze and curl around like smoke the sides and edges of perfectly unexpected associations. With Yusef Komunyakaa's *Talking Dirty To The Gods* in mind, I circle all the way back to Geoffrey Chaucer, to *The Canterbury Tales*, which has been set to hip-hop by Baba Brinkman, an Ontario performance artist who recognizes how closely Chaucer's lines and rhymes — to say nothing of bombast and bawdiness — resemble English spoken-word poetry today. Brinkman's *The Rap Canterbury Tales* picks up the beat where the 14th century bard left off.

My point of course is that all the lives we lead, lead to poetry again and again. Why at memorial services, funerals, weddings, showers, christenings — virtually at any event that marks an essential life passage — do we inevitably turn to a poem or a scripture passage to express the giant loss, the giant hurt, the giant gain, the giant change, gigantic silence?

In this indescribably alluring silence that hangs between real-life lovers and warriors poetry builds up. The late Kenneth Patchen, a mid-20th century American poet who performed his work with Charles Mingus and other jazz masters, loads up his deathless poem ("In Your Body All Bodies Lie") with the line: "Your native zone is silence." It is in and against and from this uninterruptible pregnancy of silence and emptiness that all discourse emerges. In a quiet car parked at lakeshore or seashore, on a night so full and hot with moon you can almost forget we reside in a universe vast enough to harbor all the children of children of children of children of children of children of children of children of children of children of children of children to the trillionth power — and then some. There's something that's been building up inside you for so long that all you can do now is belt or ooze it out in poetry.

That's one viewpoint. It happens to be a viewpoint that takes into consideration the post-Romantic notion that poetry is all about me and me and me and maybe a little bit of you and the rest of the world. Before the Romantics — Britain's Byron, Shelley, Coleridge, Keats — poetry spoke for the world. It did the whole world's dirty work of remembering and keeping dates straight ("Thirty days hath September, / April, June, and November"). Poetry narrated history ("Led on, and second all the armament / Followed them forth; and meanwhile there was heard / A mighty shout: 'Come, O ye sons of Greeks, Make free your country, make your children free'" — Aeschylus). Poetry instructed ("Forgetting that the Self exists, / That is the mind's greatest joy," from one of the ancient Chinese poet Li Po's ecstatic poems about the curative effects of wine, and then comes Ovid's *The Art Of Love* or Baltasar Gracián's *The Art Of Worldly Wisdom*). And poetry reported ("So, naturalists observe, a flea / Has smaller fleas that on him prey; / And these have smaller still to bite 'em; / And so proceed, ad infinitum," from "Poetry, A Rhapsody"). This is how the prescient Jonathan Swift (1667-1745) already understood those self-replicating systems that pioneering chaos theorist Benoit Mandelbrot and mathematicians who followed call fractals.

As a self-replicating species, believed now to be descended from one African Adam and Eve, we might do well to dwell on a time when there was no laptop, no iPod, no DVD, no cell phone, no digicam, no PDA, no CD, no e-mail, no Internet, no TV, no radio, no world stage, no Star Quest. We were all there was. Communities of people — however small, however big — with our bodies, our arms and legs, our faces, our faculties, our souls, our beating hearts and our vibrant, feeling-filled voices. That was it. Take away painting, take away music, take away drama, take away film, take away sculpture, take away storytelling, take away dance — and here we'd still have it all in the form of poetry, its rhythms, the sound of it, the pictures it delivers, the tales it tells, the shapes it forms, its silences and mysteries.

While language poets, concrete poets and other visually oriented poets may take issue, I'm willing to go on record in saying that the human body is indeed the perfect instrument for poetry. With voice and ear as two-way transmitter, how can it miss its timeless target? As you listen to the unsilenced voices of these many poets, soak and float in the sounds poetry makes. Listen to how our many selves sound. How else would you say these things?

Al Young is Poet Laureate of California and the author of more than 20 books, which include poetry, novels and essays. Among others, his honors include Guggenheim, Fulbright and NEA Fellowships, two American Book Awards and two Pushcart Prizes. Young has taught at such universities as Stanford, U.C. Santa Cruz and the University of Michigan. He lives in Berkeley.

OUR LIVES DISTILLED
by REBEKAH PRESSON MOSBY

"The genius of poetry is not related to time. Poetry does not follow science. Poetry doesn't get better as time passes by. Science gets better, but poetry does not."

— *Derek Walcott*

If there was ever a time when the world needed poetry, this is it. Often we think of poetry as the expression of our best selves: ourselves in love or victorious in a righteous struggle (think World War II, Civil Rights or the World Series). We might even pen an ode to celebrate reaching a milestone such as marriage, graduation or the birth of a child.

But great poets take on all of life's experiences, including loss, grief, mourning and just plain sadness. It's not that poets have answers for the suffering caused by such life-changing events as 9/11, the tsunami in Indonesia, Hurricanes Katrina and Rita, earthquakes in Pakistan, terrorist attacks abroad like the bombings in London and Madrid or the war in Iraq. And it's not that they can change the unrest and uncertainty that we all face these days, but it is true that poets have insight into the human heart, that they can help us understand ourselves and the others around us — and that is an enormous comfort.

Poetry, as Gwendolyn Brooks said, is "life distilled." Poetry is also language and experience distilled. Most poetry is not written to tell the news as journalism but rather to

HALF a league,
half a league,
Half a league onward,
All in the valley of Death
Rode the six hundred.
"Forward, the Light Brigade!
Charge for the guns!" he said:
Into the valley of Death
Rode the six hundred.

"**FORWARD** the Light Brigade**!**"

Was there a man dismay'd ?
Not tho' the soldier knew
Some one had blunder'd:
Theirs not to make reply,
Theirs not to reason why,
Theirs but to do and die:
Into the valley of **Death**
Rode the **6** h u n d r e d.

Cannon to right of them,
Cannon to left of them,
Cannon in front of them
Volley'd and thunder'd;
Storm'd at with shot and shell,
Boldly they rode and well,
Into the jaws of Death,
Into the mouth of Hell
Rode the six hundred.

"The Charge Of The Light Brigade"
by Alfred, Lord Tennyson

Flash'd all their sabres bare,
Flash'd as they turn'd in air
Sabring the gunners there,
Charging an army, while
All the world wonder'd:
Plunged in the battery-smoke
Right thro' the line they broke;
Cossack and Russian
Reel'd from the sabre-stroke
Shatter'd and sunder'd.
Then they rode back, but not
Not the six hundred.

Cannon to right of them,
Cannon to left of them,
Cannon behind them
Volley'd and thunder'd;
Storm'd at with shot and shell,
While horse and hero fell,
They that had fought so well
Came thro' the jaws of Death,
Back from the mouth of Hell,
All that was left of them,
Left of six hundred.

When can their glory fade?
O the wild charge they made!
All the world wonder'd.
Honor the charge they made!
Honor the Light Brigade,
Noble six hundred!

They dragged you from the homeland,
They chained you in coffles,
They huddled you spoon-fashion in filthy hatches,
They sold you to give a few gentlemen ease.

"STRONG MEN" by Sterling A. Brown
(excerpt)

reflect upon it, to consider its implications to our lives and its effect on the human heart. In "Parsley," Rita Dove's poem about the cruelties of the former dictator of the Dominican Republic, Miguel Trujillo, and Carolyn Forché's recollection in "The Colonel," of a dinner with an unnamed colonel who trots out his collection of human ears after an opulent meal, we feel the terror, and perhaps some of the pain, of the victims of these men's crimes many years after the events. By the same token, Deborah Garrison's poem "I Saw You Walking," about a survivor of the World Trade Center attack trying to get home, makes us want to cheer and kiss the man's dusty, torn clothing.

These poems of witness help us understand the suffering in the world, but every great poem brings out some heightened emotion, some sense of humanity that can only be achieved through art. Even poems that make us laugh out loud, such as Ogden Nash's "Portrait Of The Artist As A Prematurely Old Man" and Lawrence Ferlinghetti's "See it was like this when…" and "Underwear" and John Ashbery's "My Philosophy Of Life," tell us something about our way of living in the world — about what makes us different from the other animals and like each other.

Taking such an unguarded look at life can be a double-edged sword. We all know that there is a measure of consolation in working through one's feelings on a subject, and art therapy is now widely prescribed for patients with all sorts of emotional problems. But close encounters with the darkest reaches of the soul can also be hazardous to one's emotional and even physical health. Even in the fifth century B.C. Hippocrates used the term *melancholia* (in English, *melancholy*) to describe a state of sadness or, literally, "black bile." In the fifth century A.C., early Christians referred to a condition known as acédie, which is roughly translated as an irritation or anxiety of the heart. The arts have always been used to express these conditions, which have gradually evolved over time to describe psychological conditions such as depression or bipolar disorder, rather than to define religious experiences. A recent exhibition in Paris traced visual artists' depictions of these states, but they have also been the subject of poets since the dawn of the written word.

As far back as the Greek poet Homer, the seer Cassandra was tormented and damned by visions of the future, and sometimes it seems that many poets suffer the same fate.

It is certainly true that many poets have been the victims of depression and mental illness, manifesting in a variety of ways from alcoholism and drug abuse (notably Dylan Thomas, Charles Bukowski and Jack Kerouac) to suicide (John Berryman, Sylvia Plath and Anne Sexton).

And the heightened awareness that comes with such close and fearless observation has also led many poets to bear severe consequences from society for their beliefs. Muriel Rukeyser and Sylvia Plath were often ridiculed for treating women's concerns such as menstruation and childbirth as serious subjects for poetry. William Stafford and Robert Lowell were conscientious objectors in World War II. Stafford worked in alternative service camps and Lowell spent time in prison. Yet while both shared an inability to fight in a war, they were very different humans and very different poets. Lowell's vision of life, like Plath's, was largely tragic and both wrote confessional poetry that turned inward. Though Stafford and Rukeyser wrote of personal experience as well, both wrote verse that often turned to politics and were able to do so with a deft touch and a sense of optimism.

But this collection is not about analyzing the character of the poets themselves, but rather enjoying the power of their words. When we listen to a poet reading his or her own work we benefit not simply from the poem's beauty and the wisdom behind it, but we also get to know the poet in a very real, almost tangible way. Nearly all serious poets give thoughtful consideration to the music and rhythm of a poem, and many read aloud to themselves while writing. Thus, when we hear a poem

Passing Remark
by William Stafford

In scenery I like flat country.
    In life I don't like much to happen.
        In personalities I like mild colorless people.
    And in colors I prefer gray and brown.

**My wife, a vivid girl from the mountains,
    says,**

"THEN WHY DID YOU CHOOSE ME?"

mildly I lower my brown eyes —
there are so many things admirable people
do not understand.

read by its author, we learn what music the poet intended it to have. We also learn what the poet sounds like, how he or she breathes and, on occasion, catch the poet in an unguarded, telling moment of emotional vulnerability — all helping give weight to the poem's message.

Poetry, of course, predates recording technology; in fact, it predates writing by thousands of years. No doubt, some of the first words spoken were used to express a poem. The first poems we know of date back 3,000 to 4,000 years and were written down much later. Initially, poems were always spoken and certain members of a society were entrusted with memorizing the poems. Traveling performers in Greece passed on Homer's tale of the Trojan War, the *Iliad*, and Babylonians recited the adventures of the Sumerian hero Gilgamesh. These poems were not simply artworks; they were the history of a people.

Memorizing a poem that would later fill hundreds of pages in a book was no small feat; however, it was made somewhat easier by the use of rhyme and meter. The rhyme scheme used by Homer, dactylic hexameter, is also used by Nobel Laureate Derek Walcott in his brilliant Caribbean epic, *Omeros*, a brief excerpt of which he reads here.

Formal structures have always made memorizing poetry easier, and in the 19th century reading and performing poetry was a common after-dinner family pastime. Until the middle of the 20th century most schoolchildren could recite many poems, among them, the first heard on this collection, Tennyson's tribute to the doomed soldiers of the Crimean War, "The Charge Of The Light Brigade."

Poetry On Record: 98 Poets Read Their Work (1888-2006) in fact starts with three poets recorded by Edison himself. Edison's brilliance extended beyond his invention of the phonograph; he also had the presence of mind to immediately make recordings of many of the important voices of his time. Shortly after developing a means of transferring voices to a wax cylinder, he sent recording equipment to England where the voices of the most famous poets of the time, those of Alfred, Lord Tennyson and Robert Browning, were captured while the poets were grand old men.

Despite remastering, these recordings still sound like they are some 118 years old. Unless you know the Tennyson, Browning and Whitman poems by heart, it's best to start out by listening while reading them in the enclosed book as they may initially sound like gibberish to the ear accustomed to digital sound quality. Tennyson's recitation of his most famous poem still sends shivers up the spine as the 79-year-old poet intones his familiar phrases.

Although the words are difficult to make out, the excitement in Robert Browning's voice as he speaks is palpable. Browning is so overcome by his involvement with this cutting-edge technology that he stumbles over a poem he has, no doubt, recited many times and has to start again. His recitation is followed by three cheers from the other men in the room who are equally caught up.

Of the three Edison recordings, only the one of the American giant of modern poetry, Walt Whitman, has had its authenticity questioned. We know that Edison wished to record Whitman, and we know that Whitman (who was so tireless a self-promoter that he once reviewed his own book!) would have liked to be recorded. His four-line poem, "America," published in the 1889 edition of *Leaves Of Grass*, seems too obscure to be chosen by a forger. As Galway Kinnell points out, Whitman wanted to be seen as more patriotic and acceptable to the general public late in his life, which is why he wrote such work as "America." Still, the original wax cylinder has never been found and neither has any documentation verifying that the recording session took place. Kinnell, who says he is unsure of the recording's authenticity, also says that the first time he heard it, a flock of birds flew to the ceiling of the church he was in at the moment Whitman's voice hit the air.

A Blessing
(excerpt)

```
For she has walked over to me
And nuzzled my left hand.
She is black and white,
Her mane falls wild on her forehead,
And the light breeze moves me to caress her long ear
That is delicate as the skin over a girl's wrist.
Suddenly I realize
That if I stepped out of my body I would break
Into blossom.
```

by James Wright

By the time we reach the recordings of William Butler Yeats, recording technology has improved dramatically, but the style of reading still hails to the 19th century, when readings were often held in theaters before large audiences that required the performer to project his or her voice to the upper balconies without amplification. Yeats' style of reading, which fellow Irish Nobel Laureate Seamus Heaney calls an "elevated chant," was controversial even in his own time. However, Yeats makes quite clear that he has given the matter some thought and says, "I will not read [my poems] as if they were prose." He then goes on to read his best-known poem, "The Lake Isle Of Innisfree," a poem that is echoed in Seamus Heaney's own memory of childhood, "Death Of A Naturalist."

Yeats' style of chanting seems to have had a profound effect on at least one other poet. Listening to Ezra Pound read, he sounds for all the world like an Irishman, rather than an American from Hailey, Idaho. While other poets may not imitate Yeats' Irish accent, the type of very dramatic and highly cadenced delivery he brings to a poem can be heard in many other readings, including those by Edna St. Vincent Millay, Sterling Brown and, of course, Dylan Thomas.

> "I don't think of the meaning (of poems) as much as pleasure —
> as if I were listening to Schubert, whose phrases move my
> heart. Poems are pure music, poets are possessed. That's why
> it appeals to me."
>
> — *William Maxwell*

Gertrude Stein once told an interviewer who questioned whether her experimental writing made sense, "Everything I write means exactly what it says" and added, "If you like my writing, you understand it." Listening to her poetic portrait of Picasso, it's easy to hear what she means. Although modernism had thoroughly penetrated the world of visual art by the turn of the 20th century, Stein was well ahead of her time with her linguistic version of modernism that placed words according to their sounds, rather than their meanings.

Later Modernists, including T.S. Eliot, Ezra Pound and H.D., wrote poems that were peppered with references to classical and Continental languages and culture and yet often seemed to defy narrative sense and even meaning (though many scholars have devoted their careers to decoding the meanings of each word written by these poets), all the while full of immense lyrical power and strewn with such unforgettable phrases as "I grow old... I grow old... /I shall wear the bottoms of my trousers rolled," from Eliot's "The Love Song Of J. Alfred Prufrock."

Understanding Robert Frost's lyrics was never a problem. There have been times when Frost's understated, very American

America
by Walt Whitman

Centre of **EQUAL DAUGHTERS**, **EQUAL SONS**,

All, all alike **ENDEAR'D**, **GROWN**, **UNGROWN**, **YOUNG** or **OLD**,

STRONG, **AMPLE**, **FAIR**, **ENDURING**, **CAPABLE**, **RICH**,

Perennial with **THE EARTH**, with **FREEDOM**, **LAW** + **LOVE**,

A **GRAND**, **SANE**, **TOWERING**, **SEATED** Mother,

Chair'd in the adamant of Time.

voice has been dismissed as a bit too simple, but those critics are overwhelmed by the vast majority of us who find profound truth in a line such as "I took the one less traveled by,/And that has made all the difference."

Although Robert Frost was recorded many times (there are nearly 50 recordings of him in the Library of Congress — most of live readings), he did not warm to the studio environment in quite the same way as Carl Sandburg, who seemed born to the microphone. Sandburg was a professional singer, as well as a poet and, like Yeats, he tended to chant his poems. Sandburg also had the presence of mind to alter his poems as he read them. For example, in a recording of his 1918 poem, "Grass," Sandburg added a then-contemporary World War II reference, "Stalingrad," to a list of World War I battle sites.

The practice of altering a poem for a recording or reading is one that persists throughout recording history. Sometimes it happens because a poem is recorded before the poem is finished, as was the case with a Library of Congress recording made by Anne Sexton before the publication of her 1960 book, *To Bedlam And Part Way Back*. Other times, as with Galway Kinnell's "After Making Love We Hear Footsteps," the poet has revised the poem over the years and even published various versions.

While artists such as Eliot, Pound and H.D. were establishing their credentials as expatriate leaders of the avant-garde and peppering their poems with references to European history and culture, many Black American artists and writers were creating their own cultural phenomenon, which came to be known as the Harlem Renaissance. Unlike their Modernist peers, the poets of the Harlem Renaissance, for the most part, wrote traditional, lyric poetry. What made the works subversive were the strata of meaning, often hidden, and the celebration of Black culture and Black life.

From this era we have Langston Hughes' embrace of his African heritage, "The Negro Speaks Of Rivers," and James Weldon Johnson's playful, yet reverential retelling of

African American folklore in "The Creation." Nearly 100 years later poems such as Sterling Brown's anthem "Strong Men" might seem to be tame, even commonplace pronouncements of Black pride, but when you think that in the 1920s the Ku Klux Klan was actively lynching hundreds of Blacks in the South and that the United States Congress repeatedly refused to so much as pass anti-lynching legislation, it is clear that any statement of Black pride was a bold one.

Edna St. Vincent Millay and Dorothy Parker, the "New Women" of the literary world, also hid subversive messages in formal rhyme. Their cynicism toward love and the traditional roles of women might have been more shocking had they not been cloaked in the disguise of a sonnet (Millay) or light verse (Parker).

Contemporary poets tend to be more open and sometimes even strident in expressing their political beliefs and demands. Marge Piercy's poem about abortion, "Right To Life," is a rant, demanding freedom of choice, as is Anne Waldman's semi-comic protest against nuclear energy, "Uh Oh Plutonium." The section of Carl Sandburg's book-length poem, *The People, Yes*, that is read here begins with "The big fish eat the little fish." Immediately, we know Sandburg is not talking about fish. On the other hand, William Stafford's recollection of taking a stand in the Civil Rights Movement in "Serving With Gideon" is quiet and modest.

The sole living poet on the first disc is Stanley Kunitz, who was 100 years old as of this writing. In "King Of The River" Kunitz compares an old man to a salmon who has spent his life fighting to get upstream. This role, as sage poetic advisor to one facing death, is also played by David Ignatow, who died five years after writing the brief elegies contained here as well as by Dylan Thomas in "And Death Shall Have No Dominion" and "The Tombstone Told When She Died," Denise Levertov in "Death Psalm: O Lord Of Mysteries," Sharon Olds in "Wonder" and Theodore Roethke in "Elegy For Jane." In her poem about abortion, "The Mother," Gwendolyn Brooks imagines a

THE LOST PILOT

*If I could cajole
you to come back for an evening,
down from your compulsive*

*orbiting, I would touch you,
read your face as Dallas,
your hoodlum gunner, now,*

*with the blistered eyes, reads
his braille editions. I would
touch your face as a disinterested*

*scholar touches an original page.
However frightening, I would
discover you...*

by James Tate

for my father, 1922-1944
(excerpt)

woman who speaks to her aborted fetus, telling it of the life they might have had.

The other great theme of literature is, of course, love, and love works its way into many poems that aren't specifically about love and many that are, including William Meredith's magnificent tribute, "Crossing Over," in which the perils of love are compared to Eliza's crossing of the ice in *Uncle Tom's Cabin*. Once again, the message is slightly subversive as we now know that Meredith's love was for another man. It is also perhaps prescient, as it was written well before the age of AIDS.

While Meredith and Richard Wilbur in "Love Calls Us To The Things Of This World" celebrate romantic love, Galway Kinnell, in "Last Gods" and Theodore Roethke, in "I Knew A Woman," deal with sexual love in ways that just might make one blush. Both poets give readings that heighten the sense of ecstasy conveyed by their poems.

In "A Blessing," James Wright feels a powerful, possibly spiritual connection to a horse and in "Lovesong," Ted Hughes takes a hard look at the joys and sorrows of the emotion as does E.E. Cummings in "as freedom is a breakfastfood." Luci Tapahonso lends a comic tale to the subject, resonant with the truth of many women's lives in "Raisin Eyes," about a woman who can't seem to rid herself of a handsome, no-good, Tony Lama-wearing Indian cowboy.

Sex and its potential consequences is the theme of D.A. Powell's roller coaster ride of a poem, "[morning broke on my cabin inverted, tempest in my forehead]." Powell, who is HIV positive, packs what seems like a lifetime into a poem about love, lust, aging and illness.

A number of the poems here are anthems of one sort or another. Most of us know Langston Hughes' stirring lyric "My soul has grown deep like the rivers" as well as Sterling Brown's mantra, "The strong men keep coming." There is Adrienne Rich's 1973 coming out poem, "Diving Into The Wreck," as well as Gwendolyn Brooks' short, quotable exploration of urban life, "We Real Cool" — and, of course, the ultimate description of a dysfunctional family, Sylvia Plath's Daddy."

Perhaps the biggest and maybe the best dysfunctional family poem of all is Allen Ginsberg's "America." In this reading, made in Berkeley, California, just after the poem was written, Ginsberg gives a hilarious, crowd-pleasing rendition of his Cold War anthem, chiding his homeland and promoting anarchy.

Of course, family can mean many things, starting with the nuclear family, which is the focus of Li-Young Lee's "My Father, In Heaven, Is Reading Out Loud," Kevin Young's "The Slaughter," Marilyn Chin's "The Floral Apron," Gloria Vando's "Fire," Robert Hayden's tribute to his stepfather, "Those Winter Sundays" and Anne Sexton's chilling "All My Pretty Ones." Then there is the larger family, or possibly tribe. In Luis Rodriguez's wrenching "The Concrete River," he recalls the small and fatalistic world he and other Latinos inhabited during the poet's youth. Juan Felipe Herrera tells of a different sort of Chicano youth in "Logan Heights And The World." The reasons for the self-destructive behavior Rodriguez witnesses are explored in Pedro Pietri's brilliant rant, "Puerto Rican Obituary."

By the same token, Adrian Louis contrasts the glorious history of Native Americans past to the often sordid conditions of the present in his powerful poems, "The Fine Printing On The Label Of A Bottle Of Non-Alcohol Beer" and "The Sweat Lodge." The dichotomies of Native American life in contemporary America are also explored by Elise Paschen in "Two Standards" and by Simon Ortiz in "Sometimes It's Better To Laugh 'Honest Injun'."

In a sense, these poems, along with Peter Balakian's "The History Of Armenia" and Audre Lorde's "Dahomey" can also be regarded as poems of witness, as the poet's observations add to our understanding not only of family and tribe but also of history and the realities of life outside the so-called mainstream of American life.

(excerpt)

I think of Wind and her wild ways the year we had nothing to lose and lost it anyway in the cursed country of the fox.

We still talk about that winter, how the cold froze imaginary buffalo on the stuffed horizon of snowbanks. Grace. The haunting voices of the starved and mutilated broke fences, crashed our thermostat dreams, and we couldn't stand it one more time. So once again we lost a winter in stubborn memory, walked through cheap apartment walls, skated through fields of ghosts into a town that never wanted us, in the epic search for grace.

– *Joy Harjo*

Of course, most any good poem means more than one thing and often more than two or three or ten. On first glance, many poems here seem to be simply close observations and, certainly, they are impressive on that level alone. Wallace Stevens' poem about a painting "So And So Reclining On Her Couch" also contains clues to his philosophy of poetry; in a more subtle sense, so do Elizabeth Bishop's "The Fish" and William Carlos Williams' "The Red Wheelbarrow." It is pretty easy to tell that W.H. Auden's "The Cave Of Nakedness" is more than a description of a bedroom.

Even more ordinary objects are celebrated in Erica Jong's "Ode To My Shoes" and A.R. Ammons' "Still," which deems the lowliest object of all — shit — worthy of admiration and appreciation.

The quotidian is also the focus of John Updike's "An Oddly Lovely Day Alone," in which the writer discovers the joys of solitude and Muriel Rukeyser's "The Ballad Of Orange And Grape," in which the poet emphasizes the chaos that can ensue when language is misused.

"Woodchucks," Maxine Kumin's much-anthologized poem about shooting the critters eating her garden, is echoed in Lucille Clifton's chilling *"cruelty. don't talk to me about cruelty,"* in which the narrator tells of her massacre of cockroaches. It is no coincidence that both poems evoke the Nazi holocaust.

Conflicts on a much larger scale are the subject of several war poems, starting with Tennyson and continuing with a portion of Stephen Vincent Benét's long poem about the Civil War, "John Brown's Body" and Joseph Brodsky's imagined conversation following the Trojan War, "Odysseus To Telemachus." Two poets write of their father's horrifying experiences in war: James Tate in "The Lost Pilot" about World War II and Suji Kwock Kim, whose father fought in the Korean War in "Fragments Of The Forgotten War." In "Facing It," Vietnam veteran Yusef Komunyakaa comes to terms with his experience while visiting the Vietnam memorial in Washington, D.C.

The ode, or tribute poem, is of course, among the oldest and most revered forms, and it finds many incarnations here. In addition to the many odes to family mentioned, there is Hayden Carruth's moving memory of writer Raymond Carver, "Ray," Elizabeth Alexander's fantasy "After The Gig: Mick Jagger" and Richard Howard's gossipy, imaginary poem about meeting Wallace Stevens (who never traveled abroad) in France, "Even In Paris." In another imagined historical scenario, Lisel Mueller's "Monet Refuses The Operation," the great painter, like Oedipus and King Lear before him, recognizes that, in order to "see," he must first be blind.

The persona poem is not always told in the voice of a real historical person. Paul Zimmer invents a character named "Zimmer" in many poems, including his delightful "Zimmer Imagines Heaven." John Berryman's creation from *77 Dream Songs* is Henry, and Charles Simic's narrator in these three short poems has no name but speaks of a series of adventures so extraordinary, they seem to be a dream.

Great poets are always aware of those that went before and the ars poetica, or poem about poetry, is also a part of the poetic tradition. The two ars poetica here, Mark Strand's "The Poem," and David Ray's "The Greatest Poem In The World," are both wry takes on the internal and external struggles of trying to make a great poem that will be widely read.

Music has also been a part of poetry from the beginning. Only a few contemporary songwriters can honestly be called poets, among them, Carl Hancock Rux, whose smooth baritone delivers his "Eleven More Days."

Jazz has long been a source of inspiration for poets and here we find Jack Kerouac reciting some of his "American Haikus" with accompaniment by Zoot Sims. Amiri Baraka uses his voice as an instrument in three short jazz poems, "Bang, Bang Outishly," "Rhythm Blues" and "Shazam Doowah." Al Young's paean to Lester Young, "Lester Leaps In," pairs with his memories of Black nationalism in "A Dance For Militant

HOW THEY BROUGHT THE GOOD NEWS from GHENT to AIX

by Robert Browning

1

I sprang to the stirrup, and Joris, and he;
I galloped, Dirck galloped, we galloped all three;
"Good speed!" cried the watch, as the gate-bolts undrew;
"Speed!" echoed the wall to us galloping through;
Behind shut the postern, the light sank to rest,
And into the midnight we galloped abreast.

2

Not a word to each other; we kept the great pace
Neck by neck, stride by stride, never changing our place;
I turned in my saddle and made its girths tight,
Then shortened each stirrup, and set the pique right,
Rebuckled the cheek-strap, chained slacker the bit,
Nor galloped less steadily Roland a whit.

Dilettantes." Joy Harjo, who speaks of a connection between early jazz and her Louisiana Indian tribe, plays saxophone on her track, "Grace."

Perhaps nothing brings out our true emotions more than the contemplation of God and religion. T.S. Eliot recalls the birth of Christ in "Journey Of The Magi," a poem that is complemented by Robert Graves' "To Juan At The Winter Solstice." John Poch recounts the life of "Simon Peter" in the voice of a true believer and Muriel Rukeyser urges Jewish pride in "To Be A Jew In The Twentieth Century." Gary Snyder captures the essence of Zen in "The Song Of The Taste." Finally, Vijay Seshadri uses an ancient Hindu myth to learn a universal truth in "The Long Meadow."

When you listen to this collection, you will laugh, cry, think, perhaps get angry and, I deeply hope, thoroughly enjoy yourself. You will also participate in the ancient tradition of oral poetry — a tradition that ties us to our ancestors and our communities and one that helps us learn how to walk in the world. There are not many models for this knowledge; most of popular culture is oriented to the commercial and is rarely produced for the benefit of the soul. Politics can make us more peaceful, healthy and wealthy, but it can't help us understand ourselves or why we are here. While religion does aim to heal the soul, it sometimes does it in ways so dogmatic that it becomes difficult for us to see the point of view of our fellow humans. Poetry has the miraculous ability to give us a small — sometimes a large — insight into our lives in the course of a few minutes and over a lifetime. And when we understand ourselves, we are much more likely to understand, tolerate and live in peace with those around us.

For my father, Don Presson, and my husband, Dewey F. Mosby

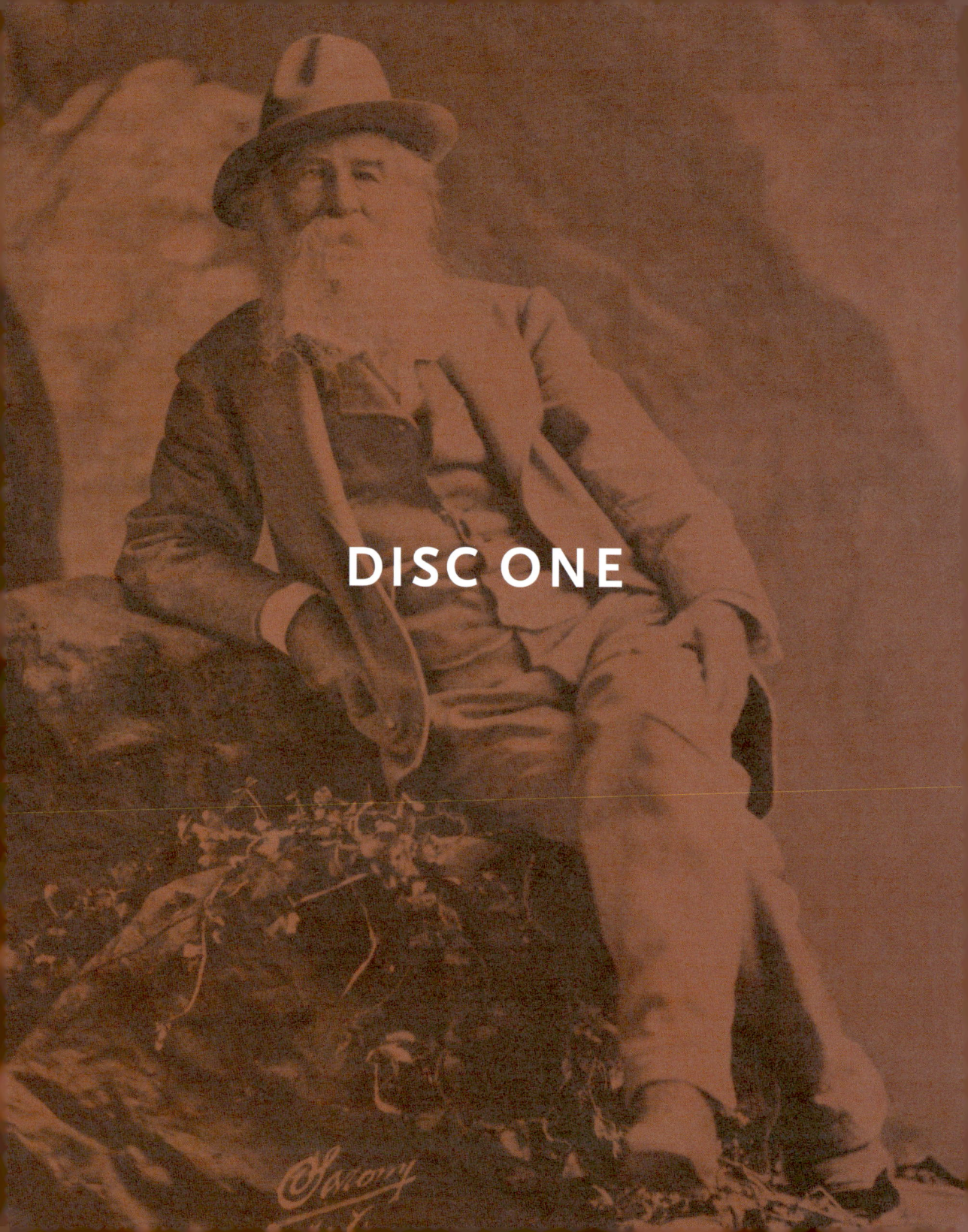

DISC ONE

ALFRED, LORD TENNYSON (1809-1892)

1. **"The Charge Of The Light Brigade"**
First appeared in *The Examiner*, December 9, 1854

2. **"Come Into The Garden, Maud"**
Originally collected in *Maud, and other poems*, 1855
Recordings made between 1890 and 1892 on wax cylinder supplied by Thomas Edison

Tennyson was among the most popular poets in Victorian England and often gave live readings to very large crowds. He succeeded William Wordsworth as Poet Laureate of England. Tennyson embodies the very best in 19th century lyric poetry.

ROBERT BROWNING (1812-1889)

3. **"How They Brought The Good News From Ghent To Aix"** (excerpt)
Library of Congress LWO 8527, reel 87
Recording made around 1889 on wax cylinder supplied by Thomas Edison

Browning, another popular Victorian poet, was married to the poet Elizabeth Barrett Browning. Known as the master of the dramatic monologue, Browning wrote *Dramatis Personnae* after the death of his wife.

WALT WHITMAN (1819-1892)

4. **"America"** (excerpt)
Originally collected in *Leaves Of Grass*, 1889
Recording believed to be made by Thomas Edison around 1889 or 1890

Whitman, along with Emily Dickinson (whose work was not known until after her death) is regarded as the first great American poet. His stunningly modern *Leaves Of Grass*, which he continually revised up until his death, still reads as a fresh document filled with energy and life.

WILLIAM BUTLER YEATS (1865-1939)

5. **"The Lake Isle Of Innisfree"**
(recorded October 28, 1937)
Originally collected in *Poems*, 1895

6. **"The Song Of The Old Mother"**
(recorded March 17, 1934)
Originally collected in *The Wind Among The Reeds*, 1899
Both recordings from Spoken Arts #753

An Irish poet, Yeats was awarded the Nobel Prize for Literature in 1923. Yeats was deeply involved in theater (he founded the Abby Theater) and in mysticism and spirituality. He is regarded by many as the greatest English language poet of the 20th century.

EDGAR LEE MASTERS (1868-1950)

7. **"Lucinda Matlock"**

8. **"Emily Sparks"**
Originally collected in *Spoon River Anthology*, 1916
Recordings from Library of Congress #T 6166-5, side A, recorded at City College of New York, 1940

Masters was a lawyer and poet whose collection of 244 poetic epitaphs, *Spoon River Anthology* (1915), won long success for its loving portrayal of a graveyard village of voices and portraits of Civil War-Era small-town America.

JAMES WELDON JOHNSON (1871-1938)

9. **"The Creation"**
Originally collected in *God's Trombones: Seven Negro Sermons In Verse*, 1927
Recorded at Columbia University, December 24, 1935

Johnson wrote songs (including "Lift Every Voice And Sing," also known as the "Negro National Anthem"), was the first Black executive secretary of the NAACP and was a diplomat in South America. His novel, *The Autobiography Of An Ex-Colored Man,* shed light on the hypocrisies of racism.

GERTRUDE STEIN (1874-1946)

10. **"If I Told Him: A Completed Portrait Of Picasso"**
Originally collected in *The Making Of Americans*, 1925
Recording from *The Spoken Arts Treasury Of 100 Modern American Poets* (SA 1040, vol. 1)

Stein was an American who spent most of her life in France, where she played hostess to the likes of Ernest Hemingway and the artists Pablo Picasso and Henri Matisse. Stein's experimental prose was modeled after Cubism, in that she used words as objects that combined to make an artwork, rather than focusing on their meaning.

ROBERT FROST (1874-1963)

11. **"The Road Not Taken"**
Originally collected in *Mountain Interval*, 1916

12. **"Stopping By Woods On A Snowy Evening"**
Originally collected in *New Hampshire*, 1923
Library of Congress #T 6117-23
Recorded live in the Coolidge Auditorium, March 27, 1941

Frost's first book of poems was published in England when he was nearly 40 years old. Frost met with immediate, lifelong success and won four Pulitzer Prizes. He wrote and read with a distinctly American voice, rejecting the tendency of the day to read and write in the British style.

CARL SANDBURG (1878-1967)

13. ***The People, Yes*** (#90) (excerpt)
Library of Congress #T 6117-47 & 48
From a lecture and reading titled "The Poet In A Democracy"
Recorded live in the Coolidge Auditorium, April 24, 1941

In addition to being a poet, Carl Sandburg was a folk singer, a songwriter, a labor activist, a politician and a historian. He won Pulitzer Prizes for the second volume of his six-volume biography of Abraham Lincoln and for his 1950 book, *Complete Poems*.

WALLACE STEVENS (1879-1955)

14. **"So And So Reclining On Her Couch"**
Originally collected in *Transport To Summer*, 1947
Recorded in front of a live audience at New York City's 92nd St. Y, January 25, 1951

Stevens led a dual existence: lawyer and insurance company executive by day and poet by night. Stevens' Symbolist-inspired, sumptuously rich and image-laden poetry has made him among America's most admired 20th century poets. In 1955 he won the National Book Award and the Pulitzer Prize for *The Collected Poems Of Wallace Stevens*.

WILLIAM CARLOS WILLIAMS (1883-1963)

15. **"The Red Wheelbarrow"**

16. **"To Elsie"**
Originally collected in *Spring And All*, 1923
Both from Library of Congress LWO 6117, side B, Tape 52

Throughout his life, Williams pursued careers as both a physician and a poet. He was close to Ezra Pound and other poets of the Imagist school but eventually decided to make his voice more associated with American culture and the richness of its language than with Europe's. Williams won a Pulitzer Prize for his last book of poems, *Pictures From Brueghel And Other Poems* (1962).

EZRA POUND (1885-1972)

17. **"Hugh Selwyn Mauberly"** (excerpt)
Originally collected in *Hugh Selwyn Mauberly*, 1920
Recording at Harvard University (call #PS3531.O82 A6 1939x)
Recorded in 1939

Pound is possibly the most influential, and most despised, American poet. He founded the Imagist school, which rejected Romanticism and looked for inspiration to "the thing." Pound was close to W.B. Yeats, T.S. Eliot, H.D. and many other titans of 20th century poetry. Yet, an avowed Fascist, he worked for Mussolini in World War II, was charged with treason and placed in a mental hospital. He died in Italy.

H.D. (1886-1961)

18. *Helen In Egypt* (excerpt), 1961
Recorded on *The Spoken Arts Treasury Of 100 Modern American Poets* (SA 1042, vol. III)

Hilda Doolittle, known as H.D., was a prominent member of Ezra Pound's group of Imagists and was once engaged to Pound. Her life was one of sexual adventure and travel. She was friends with Marianne Moore and D.H. Lawrence and was psychoanalyzed by Sigmund Freud. Although her poetry was not widely acclaimed during her lifetime, she is now considered to be an important modernist writer.

T.S. ELIOT (1888-1965)

19. **"Journey Of The Magi"** (with introduction)
Originally collected in *Collected Poems, 1909-35*
Library of Congress #T 6117-20
Recorded at the National Gallery of Art, Washington, D.C., May 23, 1947

Born in St. Louis, Missouri, Eliot eventually took British citizenship and became editor of the prestigious London publishing house Faber & Faber. Eliot is regarded as the foremost modernist poet and a leader of the avant-garde in literature. While Eliot's writing was experimental, his politics and views on religion were quite conservative. He was awarded the Nobel Prize for Literature in 1948.

EDNA ST. VINCENT MILLAY (1892-1950)

20. **"Recuerdo"**
Originally collected in *A Few Figs From Thistles*, 1922

21. **"Love Is Not All"**
Originally collected in *Fatal Interview*, 1931
Both recordings from *An Album Of Modern Poetry: An Anthology Read By The Poets*, Library of Congress PL, 20, 21, 22, 1959

St. Vincent Millay was a master of the 14-line form known as the sonnet. Her 1923 book, *The Harp Weaver And Other Poems*, won a Pulitzer, making Millay the first woman to receive the prize. Millay was a feminist and the image of the "New Woman," who wrote about and openly lived a life of sexual adventure.

Gertrude Stein

DOROTHY PARKER (1893-1967)

22. **"Résumé"**
Originally collected in *Enough Rope*

23. **"The Lady's Reward"**
Originally collected in *Death And Taxes And Other Poems*,
Collected in *An Informal Hour With Dorothy Parker*, Westminster Spoken Arts 726

A high school drop-out, Parker became a well-known writer and editor at *Vanity Fair* and *Vogue* magazines, as well as a member of the renowned literary "Round Table" that met at the Algonquin Hotel in New York. Along with Edna St. Vincent Millay, she was believed to represent the "New Woman." At the end of Parker's life she became committed to Communism and to social activism, including civil rights and feminism.

E.E. CUMMINGS (1894-1962)
24. **"as freedom is a breakfastfood"**
Library of Congress #T 2863-3
Recorded at(excerpt) the 92nd St. Y, New York City, October 20, 1959

Cummings always combined writing with art and even studied art in Paris. While Cummings' poetry is reminiscent of that of Gertrude Stein, his experiments with syntax were applauded by the general public. Cummings' work was often satirical; it is also difficult to read in a literal sense. He layered voices, which often is more effective in conveying the emotion of a poem, rather than the literal meaning.

ROBERT GRAVES (1895-1985)
25. **"To Juan At The Winter Solstice"**
Originally collected in *Poems: 1939-1945*, 1946
Audio from *Robert Graves* collected by the Academy of American Poets, 1966

Graves started writing in earnest after he was injured during World War I. When his marriage to writer Laura Riding broke up, he began writing novels, including *I, Claudius*, and its sequel, *Claudius The God And His Wife Messalina*. (During the 1970s the BBC adapted the novels into a popular television series.) Graves' later work reflected his theory of the White Goddess, which was based on the beliefs of various matriarchal societies.

STEPHEN VINCENT BENÉT (1898-1943)
26. **"John Brown's Body"** (excerpt)
Collected in *John Brown's Body*, 1928
Library of Congress #T 6117-3
Recorded live in the Coolidge Auditorium, May 29, 1941

In addition to poetry, Benét wrote novels, short stories, screenplays, radio broadcasts and a libretto for an opera. Much of his writing was based on historical events, including the long, narrative poem about the Civil War, *John Brown's Body*, for which he received the Pulitzer Prize in 1929.

Ogden Nash

STERLING BROWN (1901-1939)
27. **"Strong Men"**
Originally collected in *Southern Road*, 1932
Library of Congress #T 7400 (July 9, 1973)

Although raised middle class in Washington, D.C., and educated at Williams and Harvard Colleges, Brown was best known for his 1932 book, *Southern Road*, which chronicled the lives and folk stories of everyday African Americans and was written largely in their vernacular. Brown gave credit for his sensitivity to these subjects to his experiences teaching at a series of traditionally black colleges.

LANGSTON HUGHES (1902-1967)

28. **"The Negro Speaks Of Rivers"** (with intro)

29. **"The Weary Blues"** (with intro)
Originally collected in *The Weary Blues*, 1926
Library of Congress #T 2838

Probably the most important writer of the Harlem Renaissance, Hughes is widely held to be the first African American to earn a living as a writer. Hughes' poetry often addressed the inequities of Black life in America, as well as the everyday truths of that life. Music also infused Hughes' poetry, and he was known for poems that evoke the music and the lives of those engrossed in the world of jazz, such as those in *Montage Of A Dream Deferred* (1951).

OGDEN NASH (1902-1975)

30. **"Portrait Of The Artist As A Prematurely Old Man"**
Originally collected in *Many Long Years Ago*, 1945
Reading from Columbia Records, July 3, 1959
Library of Congress #T 2982

Ogden Nash was probably the most popular poet of his day and was a regular guest on popular radio game shows, as well as a writer for television. Nash's witty poems often contained keen observations of married life and clever rhymes, which sometimes employed made-up words.

STANLEY KUNITZ (1905-)

31. **"King Of The River"**
Originally collected in *The Wellfleet Whale And Companion Poems*, 1983
Recorded in New Jersey for broadcast on the radio program *New Letters On The Air*, 1992

Stanley Kunitz has won nearly every prize for poetry, including the Pulitzer (for his *Selected Poems, 1928-1958*). He has served as Poet Laureate of the United States (then called Consultant in Poetry) and of New York state. Kunitz is also a founder of the Fine Arts Center in Provincetown, Massachusetts, and of Poets House in New York.

W.H. AUDEN (1907-1973)

32. **"The Cave Of Nakedness"**
Originally collected in *About The House*, 1965
Recorded at the Solomon R. Guggenheim Museum, March 12, 1964

British born, Auden moved to America in 1939 and became a U.S. citizen in 1946. As a writer Auden is known for his virtuosity, his ability to master nearly every style of writing, and for his command of a multitude of subjects ranging from the spiritual to the everyday. His work often reflects a wit and a wisdom seldom seen.

THEODORE ROETHKE (1908-1963)

33. **"I Knew A Woman"**
Originally collected in *Words For The Wind*, 1958

34. **"Elegy For Jane"**
Originally collected in *The Waking*, 1953
Recording from *Words For The Wind*, Folkways Records FL 9736 (1962)

Roethke's poems are filled with sensuality and lyric power that he used to declare his love for nature and beauty. His 1948 volume, *The Lost Son And Other Poems*, is widely considered his best. At the University of Washington, Roethke taught many other poets who would become renowned, including Richard Hugo, Carolyn Kizer, David Wagoner and James Wright.

ELIZABETH BISHOP (1911-1979)

35. **"Late Air"**

36. **"The Fish"**
Both originally collected in *North & South*, 1946
Audio from Columbia Masterworks ML 4259, *Pleasure Dome*

Bishop is admired for her great technical prowess and her careful observation of everyday objects. A 1955 revision of her 1946 book, *North And South*, won Bishop a Pulitzer Prize. She also served as Poet Laureate. Often associated with poet Robert Lowell, as they were close friends, Bishop's work is quite different in that she avoided the personal in her poetry.

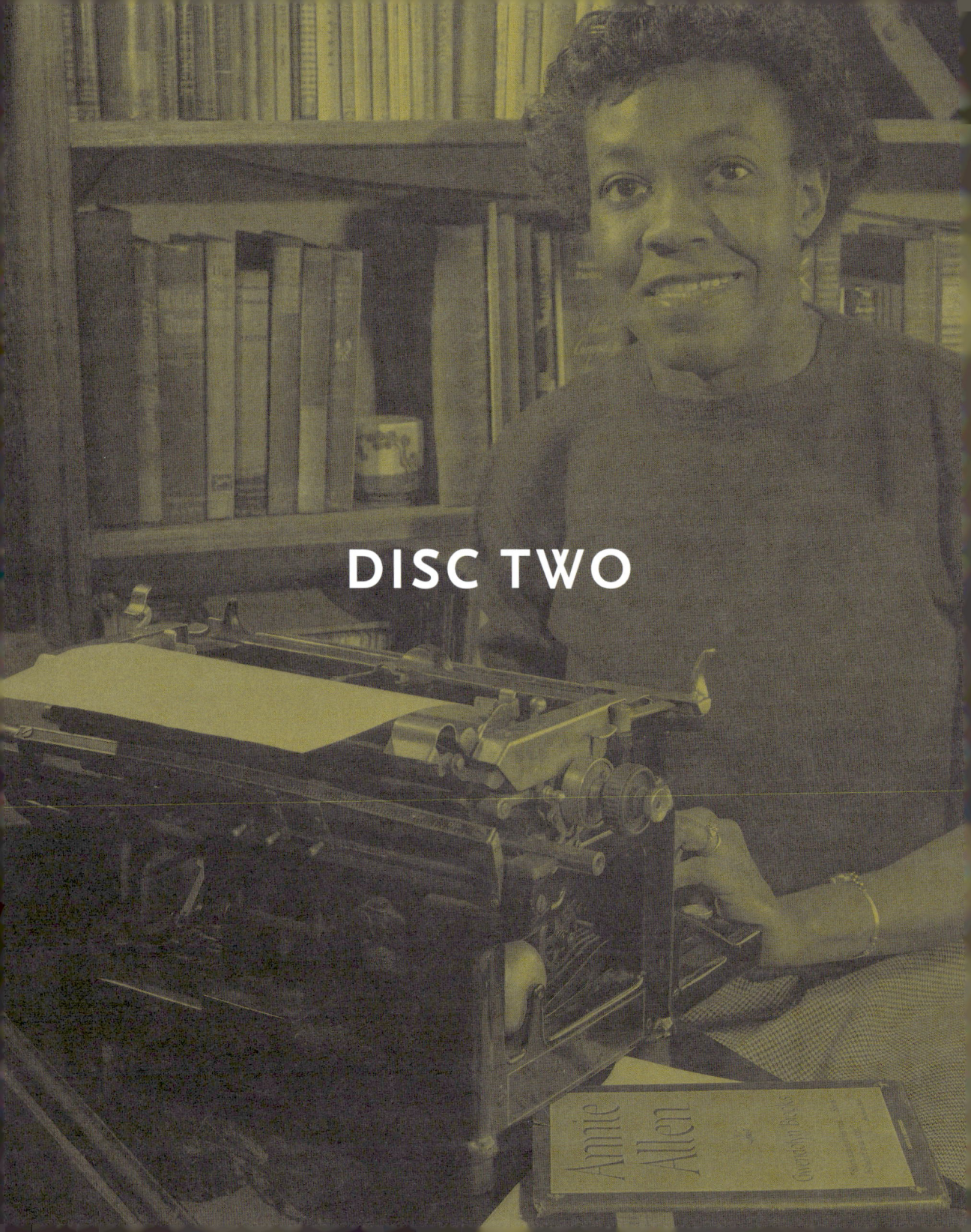
DISC TWO

ROBERT HAYDEN (1913-1982)

1. **"Those Winter Sundays"**

Originally collected in *A Ballad Of Remembrance*, 1962
Recorded at Library of Congress, February 13, 1968, #T 5266a

A student of W.H. Auden, Hayden's poetry went largely unnoticed until 1966, when he won an international poetry prize and was named Poet Laureate of Senegal. In 1975 he was also named Poet Laureate of the United States. Hayden was a practitioner of Baha'i, whose serenity, reflected in his poetry, was, at one time, widely criticized by the more political voices within the Black community.

MURIEL RUKEYSER (1913-1980)

2. **"The Ballad Of Orange And Grape"**

Originally collected in *The Speed Of Darkness*, 1968

3. **"To Be A Jew In The Twentieth Century"**

Originally collected in *Breaking Open*, 1973
Recorded at a live reading in the Folger Shakespeare Library, Washington D.C., January 21, 1974
Library of Congress #T 7679

A prolific and highly political writer, Rukeyser's work incorporated many themes, including the joys of motherhood, psychology and Greek myth. Rukeyser was once imprisoned for her anti-Vietnam War efforts. She served as a role model for feminist poets to come, including Adrienne Rich and Anne Sexton.

JOHN BERRYMAN (1914-1972)

4. **#23 ("The Lay Of Ike")**
5. **#36 ("The high ones die…")**

Originally collected in *77 Dreams Songs*, 1964
Recorded at Harvard University

Berryman's groundbreaking 1964 book, *77 Dream Songs*, made the poet a star and won him a Pulitzer Prize. In the poems, written in the voice of Berryman's alter-ego, Henry, Berryman explored a new and entirely American vernacular. But Berryman's tragic childhood (he witnessed his father's suicide at age 11) and alcoholism soon caught up with him, and he committed suicide by throwing himself off a bridge.

DAVID IGNATOW (1914-1997)

6. **"The world is so difficult to give up…"**
7. **"This is the solution, to be happy with slaughter…"**
8. **"Here I am with mike in hand, shooting down the rapids…"**
9. **"I killed a fly…"**
10. **"What about dying?…"**

All originally collected in *Shadowing The Ground*, 1991
Recorded at the National Public Radio Bureau, New York City, 1991

Ignatow lived most of his life in the New York City area and was known as a keen observer of urban life. In his 1991 book, *Shadowing The Ground*, Ignatow began to reflect, in an almost Zen-like way, upon his mortality and his unwillingness to face death.

WILLIAM STAFFORD (1914-1993)

11. **"Passing Remark"**

Originally collected in *The Rescued Year*, 1966

12. **"Serving With Gideon"**

Originally collected in *An Oregon Message*, 1987
From a live reading at the University of Missouri — Kansas City, 1982

Stafford was a proponent of a poetic language that is barely elevated above everyday speech. His deceptively simple lyrics often spoke of his pacifism and his ability to see the human condition clearly, to have an opinion on it and yet not to judge. Stafford won the National Book Award for *Traveling Through The Dark* (1962) and was named Poet Laureate in 1970.

DYLAN THOMAS (1914-1953)
13. **"And Death Shall Have No Dominion"**
14. **"The Tombstone Told When She Died"**
Originally collected in *Collected Poems, 1934-1952*, 1952
Recording from Library of Congress #T 5293-6, March 9, 1950

Thomas' Welsh heritage informed much of his writing, including of course, *A Child's Christmas In Wales* (published posthumously). Thomas was popular all over the English-speaking world for his dramatic style of reading, beginning with British radio broadcasts in the 1930s and continuing through several American tours in the 1950s. Thomas died of acute alcohol poisoning in New York City.

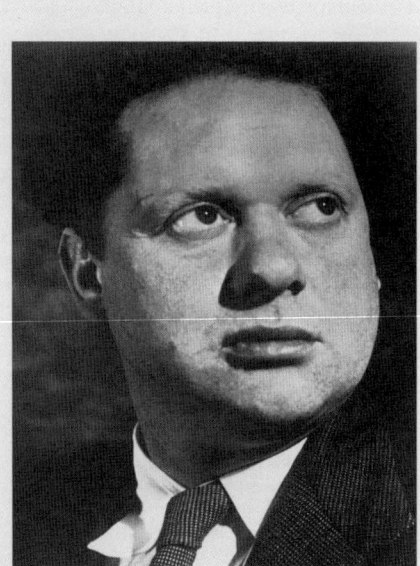
Dylan Thomas

GWENDOLYN BROOKS (1917-2000)
15. **"The Mother"**
Originally collected in *A Street In Bronzeville*, 1945
16. **"We Real Cool"**
Originally collected in *The Bean Eaters*, 1960
Recorded for *New Letters On The Air*, 1995

In 1950 Brooks became the first African American to win a Pulitzer Prize in poetry for her second book, *Annie Allen*, which, like her acclaimed first book, *A Street In Bronzeville*, contained carefully crafted observations of Black life in her native Chicago. In the 1960s Brooks became highly influenced by the Black Arts Movement and started publishing only with Black-owned publishing companies. Brooks was named Poet Laureate in 1985.

ROBERT LOWELL (1917-1977)
17. **"Skunk Hour"**
Originally collected in *Life Studies*, 1959
Recording from Library of Congress #T 3188, October 31, 1960

Lowell won a Pulitzer Prize for his second book of poems, *Lord Weary's Castle* (1946), but it was his fourth volume, published in 1959, *Life Studies*, that transformed the poetry world with what came to be known as "Confessional" or autobiographical poetry. Lowell later won a second Pulitzer for 1973's *The Dolphin*.

WILLIAM MEREDITH (1919-)
18. **"Crossing Over"**
Originally collected in *The Cheer*, 1980
Recorded at the Library of Congress

Meredith's first book, 1944's *Love Letter From An Impossible Land*, was chosen for the Yale Series of Younger Poets Award while the author was a Navy pilot during World War II. Meredith has since won many prizes, including the Pulitzer for his 1987 book, *Partial Accounts: New And Selected Poems*. He served as Poet Laureate from 1978-1980.

LAWRENCE FERLINGHETTI (1919-)
19. **"See it was like this when…"**
20. **"Underwear"**
Originally collected in *A Coney Island Of The Mind*, 1958
Recorded at The Writer's Center, Bethesda, MD
From the album *Lawrence Ferlinghetti: Into The Deeper Pools*, Watershed Foundation #WTC-167, 1984

A close associate of the Beat poets, Ferlinghetti cofounded San Francisco's renowned **City Lights** bookstore. Ferlinghetti published Ginsberg's groundbreaking book, *Howl And Other Poems* (1956), and successfully defended it against obscenity charges. Ferlinghetti's 1958 *A Coney Island Of The Mind* shows the poet's deft and often cutting wit.

CHARLES BUKOWSKI (1920-1995)
21. **"The Secret Of My Endurance"**
Originally collected in *Dangling In The Tournefortia*, 1981
Recorded at the Sweetwater, Redondo Beach, CA, April 1980
From the album *Hostage,* Freeway #1058, 1985

Something of a cult figure for the disenfranchised, Bukowski's work often documented and sometimes celebrated his own rough and tumble early life of menial jobs and alcoholism. Bukowski sometimes wrote in the voice of an alter ego, Henry Chinaski.

HAYDEN CARRUTH (1921-)
22. **"Ray"**
Originally collected in *Collected Shorter Poems: 1946-1991*, 1992
Recorded in the author's home, 1996

Carruth is a widely published essayist and critic, as well as a poet. In his life and work, Carruth celebrates rural life and often takes a strong political and moral stance. His 1996 book, *Scrambled Eggs And Whiskey*, won the National Book Award. Carruth is retired from his post at Syracuse University and lives in upstate New York.

Dorothy Parker

RICHARD WILBUR (1921-)
23. **"Love Calls Us To The Things Of This World"**
Originally collected in *Things Of This World: Poems By Richard Wilbur*, 1956
Recorded for *New Letters On The Air*, 1990

In the 1950s Wilbur was regarded as the first among equals for his witty, smoothly written poetry. His 1956 *Things Of This World* won him the Pulitzer Prize and the National Book Award. Wilbur's formal approach is perhaps less valued as time goes on, but Wilbur did go on to win a second Pulitzer Prize for *New And Collected Poems* (1988).

JACK KEROUAC (1922-1969)
WITH AL COHN & ZOOT SIMMS
24. **"American Haikus"** (excerpt)
From *Book Of Haiku*, an uncollected collection, portions of which appear in *Scattered Poems*, 1971
From the album *Blues And Haikus*, Hanover #5006, 1959

Along with Allen Ginsberg, Kerouac is the most famous of the Beat writers. Kerouac's best-known work is his 1957 autobiographical novel, *On The Road*. Kerouac's haikus reflect his interest in Buddhism and in jazz music. At age 47 Kerouac died of cirrhosis of the liver.

DENISE LEVERTOV (1923-1997)
25. **"Death Psalm: O Lord Of Mysteries"**
Originally collected in *Life In The Forest*, 1978
Recorded live in Hoylston Hall, Harvard University, November 29, 1978

Levertov was born in England and moved to America — where, after World War II, during which she served as a nurse — she eventually became a citizen. Levertov's poems often find the divine in the ordinary as she ponders the mysteries of life in the voices of animals and nature.

LISEL MUELLER (1924-)
26. **"Monet Refuses The Operation"**
Originally collected in *Second Language*, 1986
Recorded in Kansas City, MO, for *New Letters On The Air*, 1981

Mueller left Nazi Germany in 1939 for America and learned English at age 15. She won a Pulitzer Prize for her 1996 collection, *Alive Together: New & Selected Poems*. In addition to her own work, Mueller sometimes translates the work of German poets.

MAXINE KUMIN (1925-)
27. **"Woodchucks"**
Recorded live at Colgate University, April 18, 1989

Kumin's work often focuses on rural life (she lives on a farm in New Hampshire); her 1972 book, *Up Country: Poems Of New England*, won the Pulitzer Prize. Kumin has served as Poet Laureate and as a Chancellor of the Academy of American Poets. In addition to poetry, she has published many children's books.

ALLEN GINSBERG (1926-1997)
28. **"America"**
Originally collected in *Howl And Other Poems*, 1956
Recorded at Town Hall Theater, Berkeley, CA, March 1956
From the album *Holy Soul Jelly Roll: Poems And Songs 1949-1993*, Rhino/Word Beat #71593, 1994

Ginsberg exploded onto the American poetry scene in 1956 with his groundbreaking poem "Howl" (see Lawrence Ferlinghetti). In addition to being among the founders of the Beat movement, Ginsberg cofounded, with Anne Waldman, the Jack Kerouac School of Disembodied Poetics at the Naropa Institute in Colorado.

A.R. AMMONS (1926-2001)
29. **"Still"**
Originally collected in *The Selected Poems: 1951-1977*, 1986
Recorded in front of a live audience at New York City's 92nd Street Y, October 28, 1996

Ammons was a prolific writer who started writing poetry aboard a naval destroyer escort in World War II. He ended his career as a professor at Cornell University. Ammons was often noted as a poet with the ability to celebrate the most lowly and ordinary objects.

JOHN ASHBERY (1927-)
30. **"My Philosophy Of Life"**
Originally collected in *Can You Hear, Bird*, 1995
Recording from *John Ashbery*, 1994, The Academy of American Poets

Ashbery is associated with the New York School of poets who combine surrealism and modernism to form an urban art form. He has won nearly every poetry prize possible. His *Self-Portrait In A Convex Mirror* (1975) received the Pulitzer Prize for Poetry, the National Book Critics Circle Award and the National Book Award.

GALWAY KINNELL (1927-)

31. **"After Making Love We Hear Footsteps"**
Originally collected in *Mortal Acts, Mortal Words*, 1980
Recorded in New York City, 1996

32. **"Last Gods"**
Originally collected in *When One Has Lived A Long Time Alone*, 1990
Recorded in Kansas City, MO, for *New Letters On The Air*, 1981

Kinnell's work is sometimes influenced by his social activism (he worked for racial equality and against the Vietnam War) and tends to have a strong spiritual dimension. He is noted for his readings, or "recitations," and has won a Pulitzer Prize for his 1980 *Selected Poems*. He teaches at NYU and divides his time between Vermont and New York.

JAMES WRIGHT (1927-1980)

33. **"A Blessing"**
Originally collected in *The Branch Will Not Break*, 1963
Library of Congress, #T 4949

Wright's poems often show sympathy for the disenfranchised, including those raised in poverty (as he was), the homeless and homosexuals. He wrote about these people in a section of new poems included in his 1971 *Collected Poems*, which was awarded a Pulitzer Prize.

ANNE SEXTON (1928-1974)

34. **"All My Pretty Ones"**
Originally collected in *All My Pretty Ones*, 62
Library of Congress #T 3146
Recorded at the Fassett Recording Studio, Boston, MA, May 1960

35. **"For My Lover, Returning To His Wife"**
Originally collected in *Love Poems*, 1969
Recorded live in the Coolidge Auditorium, October 16, 1972
Library of Congress #T 7048

Sexton, along with Robert Lowell and Sylvia Plath, is among the major poets of the Confessional movement. Sexton used poetry as therapy and wrote openly about her lovers, menstruation, abortion and other problems. Her 1966 book, *Live Or Die*, was awarded a Pulitzer Prize. Sexton lost her battle with mental illness when she committed suicide in 1974.

T.S. Eliot

DISC THREE

RICHARD HOWARD (1929-)

  1. **"Even In Paris"** (excerpt)
Originally collected in *No Traveller*, 1986
Recorded by *New Letters On The Air*

Howard is known for his dramatic monologues and for his translations from the French. His *Untitled Subjects* (1969) was awarded a Pulitzer Prize and his translation of Baudelaire's *Les Fleurs du Mal* won a 1983 American Book Award. Howard lives in New York City.

ADRIENNE RICH (1929-)

  2. **"Diving Into The Wreck"**
Originally collected in *Diving Into The Wreck*, 1973
Recorded at the University of California, Santa Cruz, 1986
From the album *Planetarium: A Retrospective 1950-1980*, Watershed Foundation #WTC-201, 1986

When Rich graduated from Radcliffe College in 1951, her first book was chosen by W.H. Auden for the Yale Series of Younger Poets. But her carefully crafted, mainstream poetry soon changed as the wife and mother developed into a feminist and lesbian. Since 1973, when Rich published *Diving Into The Wreck*, she has been widely lionized and admired by women who are inspired by her work. She lives in California.

TED HUGHES (1930-1998)

  3. **"Lovesong"**
Originally collected in *Crow*, 1971
Recorded for *Crow*, Penguin/Faber audio, 1997

Hughes was Poet Laureate of England and the husband of American poet Sylvia Plath. His most famous poetic character is the Crow, who serves as a sort of all-knowing being through which Hughes dispenses wit, wisdom and philosophy.

DEREK WALCOTT (1930-)

  4. **"Omeros"** (excerpt)
Originally collected in *Omeros*, 1990
Recorded in Kansas City, MO, for *New Letters On The Air*, 1990

A native of St. Lucia, Walcott won the Nobel Prize for literature in 1992 after the publication of his epic poem, *Omeros*, which is often compared to *The Odyssey*. In *Omeros*, a Caribbean fisherman takes an imaginary voyage to Africa. Walcott divides his time between the U.S. and the Caribbean.

GARY SNYDER (1930-)

  5. **"The Song Of The Taste"**
  6. **"Why I Take Good Care Of My Macintosh Computer"**
Unpublished
Recorded at the Capitol Hill Hotel, Washington, D.C., 1989
From the album *This Is Our Body*, Watershed Foundation #WTC-231, 1989

Snyder is known both as a member of the Beat poets and as a longtime practitioner of Zen Buddhism. His poems are usually written in the first person, generally relate a true experience, are often meditative and always show respect for the Earth. His book *Turtle Island* (1974) won the Pulitzer Prize for poetry. He is retired from the University of California at Davis.

ETHERIDGE KNIGHT (1931-1991)

  7. **"The Idea Of Ancestry"**
Originally collected in *The Essential Etheridge Knight*, 1986
Recorded at the Library of Congress, 1986
From the album *So My Soul Can Sing*, Watershed Foundation #WTC-212, 1986

Associated with the Black Arts Movement, Knight began writing poetry while serving a prison term for armed robbery, referring to prison as "my major metaphor." In 1968 he was released from prison, published his book *Poems From Prison* and married poet Sonia Sanchez. Although his work was widely acclaimed, Knight struggled all his life with a drug habit he picked up as the result of an injury suffered while fighting in the Korean War.

Allen Ginsberg

Robert Browning

SYLVIA PLATH (1932-1963)
8. **"Daddy"**
Originally collected in *Ariel*, 1965
Recorded in London, October 1962
From the album *Plath Reads,* Credo #3, 1975

Plath, who committed suicide at age 29, is widely regarded as one of the most original voices in American poetry. Her book *Ariel*, published posthumously in 1965, was edited by her husband, Ted Hughes, who was widely criticized for changing Plath's order and taking out 12 of her poems. *Ariel* has since been published in its original version with all its dark brilliance.

DAVID RAY (1932-)
9. **"The Greatest Poem In The World"**
Originally collected in *The Tramp's Cup*, 1978
Recorded in Kansas City, MO, for *New Letters On The Air*, 1979

David Ray's writings often hark back to his Depression Era childhood and the mistreatment he suffered at the hands of his family and a sexual predator who was allowed to be Ray's guardian. As a result, Ray often attempts to speak for the disenfranchised of the world. Ray lives in Tucson, Arizona, with his wife, poet Judy Ray.

JOHN UPDIKE (1932-)
10. **"An Oddly Lovely Day Alone"**
Originally collected in *Facing Nature*, 1985
Recorded at Updike's home in Massachusetts for *New Letters On The Air*, 1988

Primarily known as one of the foremost living American novelists (for which he has won two Pulitzers), Updike has written and published light verse throughout his life. He lives in Massachusetts.

AMIRI BARAKA (1934-)
11. **"Bang, Bang Outishly"**
12. **"Rhythim Blues"**
13. **"Shazam Doowah"**
Originally collected in *The Music: Reflections On Jazz And Blues*, 1987
Recorded in Kansas City, MO, for *New Letters On The Air*, 1988

Baraka first gained fame as a playwright writing under the name LeRoi Jones. In the 1960s he became perhaps the leading member of the Black Arts Movement. In addition to his Black Nationalist writings, Baraka has written extensively about jazz. He lives in New Jersey.

AUDRE LORDE (1934-1992)
14. **"Dahomey"**
Originally collected in *The Black Unicorn*, 1978
Recorded in Kansas City, MO, for *New Letters On The Air*, 1978

Like Adrienne Rich before her, Lorde moved from a traditional life (married with children) and carefully crafted poems to a life and work that embraced her lesbianism and growing political interests. Lorde's writing also focused on her ideas about race (her parents were Caribbean immigrants) and on the cancer that eventually killed her. Probably her most popular book is 1976's *The Black Unicorn.*

MARGE PIERCY (1934-)
15. "Right To Life"
Originally collected in *Circles On The Water*, 1982
Recorded in Aspen, CO, for *New Letters On The Air*, 1989

Piercy is perhaps best known for feminist novels, such as her best-seller, *Woman On The Edge Of Time* (1976). But she has also published some 17 books of poetry. Piercy's voice tends to be energetic, blunt and unafraid of conflict.

MARK STRAND (1934-)
16. "The Poem"
Originally collected in *Sleeping With One Eye Open*, 1964
Recorded in Park City, UT, at KPCW, March 1986
From the album *The Untelling*, Watershed Foundation #WTC-204, 1986

Strand is a much-lauded artist whose awards include the Pulitzer Prize for his 1998 book *Blizzard Of One*, a MacArthur "genius" grant and the Bollingen Prize. He has also served as Poet Laureate and as a Chancellor of the Academy of American Poets. He teaches in the Committee on Social Thought at the University of Chicago.

PAUL ZIMMER (1934-)
17. "Zimmer Imagines Heaven"
Originally collected in *Reunions: Selected And New Poems*, 1983
Recorded in Kansas City, MO, for *New Letters On The Air*, 1987

Zimmer is retired as Director of the University of Iowa Press in Iowa City and lives on a farm. He has published 11 books of poems, including *The Great Bird Of Love: Poems* (1989), which was selected by William Stafford for the National Poetry Series.

LUCILLE CLIFTON (1936-)
18. "*cruelty. don't talk to me about cruelty*"
Originally collected in *next*, 1987
Recorded by Rebekah Presson Mosby in San Francisco for *New Letters On The Air*, 1989

Lucille Clifton's terse, witty lyrics recall such episodes as growing up Black when Shirley Temple was all the rage. Clifton is a Chancellor of the Academy of American Poets and a former Poet Laureate of the State of Maryland. She is a Professor at St. Mary's College of Maryland. Her 2000 volume, *Blessing The Boats: New And Selected Poems 1988-2000*, won the National Book Award.

Sylvia Plath

DIANE WAKOSKI (1937-)

19. **"I Have Had To Learn To Live With My Face"**
Originally collected in *The Motorcycle Betrayal Poems*, 1971
Recorded in Kansas City, MO, for *New Letters On The Air*, 1987

A prolific writer who has published more than 40 books of poems, Wakoski is perhaps best known for her work that celebrates American life and culture. She teaches at Michigan State University in East Lansing.

CHARLES SIMIC (1938-)

20. **"We were so poor…"**

21. **"I was stolen by the gypsies…"**

22. **"Everybody knows the story…"**
Originally collected in *The World Doesn't End: Prose Poems*, 1989
Recorded in Aspen, CO, for *New Letters On The Air*, 1990

Simic was born and raised in the former Yugoslavia, and the language and culture of his youth find their way into the poems he writes in English. His 1990 book, *The World Doesn't End: Prose Poems*, was awarded the Pulitzer Prize. Simic teaches at the University of New Hampshire.

SEAMUS HEANEY (1939-)

23. **"Death Of A Naturalist"**
Originally collected in *Death Of A Naturalist*, 1966
Audio from Harvard University

Irish poet Seamus Heaney was awarded the Nobel Prize for Literature in 1995. His *Opened Ground* (1999) was named a *New York Times* Notable Book of the Year. He divides his time between Dublin and Harvard University, where he teaches part-time each year.

AL YOUNG (1939-)

24. **"Lester Leaps In"**

25. **"A Dance For Militant Dilettantes"**
Originally collected in *The Blues Don't Change*, 1982
Recorded in Kansas City, MO, for *New Letters On The Air*, 1992

Al Young lives in Berkeley and is Poet Laureate of the state of California. He is as noted for his novels and his books of essays on music as for his poetry. Young's early writings often reflected on his family's move from rural Mississippi to Detroit and his association with adherents of the Black Arts Movement. Although music has always been a central focus, Young's work has become more concerned with political issues in recent years.

Amiri Baraka

GLORIA VANDO (1939-)

26. **"Fire"**
Originally collected in *Promesas: Geography Of The Impossible*, 1993
Recorded in Kansas City, MO, for *New Letters On The Air*, 1993

Vando is a Nuyorican whose poems often speak of her childhood in New York City with an actress mother and bandleader father. Her 2002 *Shadows & Supposes* won the Poetry Society of America's Alice Fay DiCastagnola Award and the Latino Literary Award for Best Poetry Book. Vando founded the women's literary magazine *Helicon Nine* and cofounded The Writers Place in Kansas City, Missouri.

JOSEPH BRODSKY (1940-1996)

27. **"Odysseus To Telemachus"**
Originally collected in *A Part Of Speech*, 1980
Recorded in Washington, D.C., 1986
From the album *Winter,* Watershed Foundation #WTC-221, 1987

The Soviet-born poet spent 19 months in Russian labor camps before being expelled from his homeland and coming to America. Although Brodsky wrote nearly all his poems in Russian, in 1991 he became the first person to be given the title Poet Laureate of the United States (previously, the position was called Poetry Consultant to the Library of Congress). He won the Nobel Prize for Literature in 1987.

SIMON J. ORTIZ (1941-)

28. **"Sometimes It's Better To Laugh 'Honest Injun'"**
Originally collected in *Going For The Rain*, 1976
From a live reading at Colgate University, 2004

Ortiz was born and raised in New Mexico as a member of the Acuna tribe. In books such as *Woven Stone* (1992) Ortiz's poems often speak to the contradictions and even absurdities of Indian life in America. He teaches at the University of Toronto.

ERICA JONG (1942-)

29. **"Ode To My Shoes"**
Originally collected in *Becoming Light: Poems New And Selected*, 1991
From the album *Becoming Light*, Dove Audio #41810, 1992

Jong is best known as a novelist. Her classic *Fear Of Flying* (1973) was an international best-seller. But Jong has also published seven books of poems, including 1991's *Becoming Light: Poems New And Selected*. She lives in New York City.

Robert Frost

SHARON OLDS (1942-)

  1. **"Wonder"**
Originally collected in *The Father*, 1992
Recorded in New Jersey for *New Letters On The Air*, 1992

Sharon Olds was New York State Poet from 1998-2000. She teaches at NYU and lives in New York. Her book *Strike Sparks: Selected Poems* was published in 2004.

JAMES TATE (1943-)

  2. **"The Lost Pilot"**
Originally collected in *The Lost Pilot*, 1967
Recorded in Amherst, MA, for *New Letters On The Air*, 1992

Tate's first book, *The Lost Pilot* (1967), was selected for the Yale Series of Younger Poets and his *Selected Poems* (1991) won the Pulitzer Prize. Tate teaches at the University of Massachusetts in Amherst.

PEDRO PIETRI (1944-2004)

  3. **"Puerto Rican Obituary"** (excerpt)
Originally collected in *Puerto Rican Obituary*, 1973
From the album *Loose Joints*, Folkways Records FW09722 1979

Pietri was born in Puerto Rico and grew up in Harlem. He helped found the Nuyorican Poets Café. Pietri's best-known work is *Puerto Rican Obituary* (1973), in which he looks at the hardships of Nuyorican life in America.

ANNE WALDMAN (1945-)

  4. **"Uh Oh Plutonium"**
Originally collected in *Makeup On Empty Space*, 1984
Hyacinth Girls single #HG 001, 1982

Anne Waldman is often associated with the Beat poets and was a cofounder, with Allen Ginsberg, of the Jack Kerouac School of Disembodied Poetics at the Naropa Institute in Boulder, Colorado, where she directs the MFA Writing and Poetics program. *In The Room Of Never Grieve: New And Selected Poems, 1985-2003* was published in 2003.

ADRIAN LOUIS (1946-)

  5. **"The Fine Printing On The Label Of A Bottle Of Non-Alcohol Beer"**
Originally collected in *Vortex Of Indian Fevers*, 1995

  6. **"The Sweat Lodge"**
Originally collected in *The Dog Eaters*, 1992
Recorded in Kansas City, MO, for *New Letters On The Air*, 1993

Louis grew up in Nevada and is an enrolled member of the Lovelock Paiute Indian tribe. He is also a journalist who has edited four tribal newspapers. He teaches English in the Minnesota State University system.

YUSEF KOMUNYAKAA (1947-)

  7. **"Facing It"**
Originally collected in *Dien Cau Cau*, 1989
Recorded in Kansas City, MO, for *New Letters On The Air*, 1995

Komunyakaa often writes about his childhood in Bogalusa, Louisiana, and about his military service in Vietnam. His book *Neon Vernacular: New & Selected Poems 1977-1989* (1994) was awarded the Pulitzer Prize. Komunyakaa is a Chancellor of the Academy of American Poets and a professor at Princeton University.

JUAN FELIPE HERRERA (1948-)
With Mark Daterman, guitar

  8. **"Logan Heights And The World"**
Music by Mark Daterman
Originally collected in *Facegames*, 1987
Recorded at the Mt. Hood reading series, Mt. Hood, OR, 1992

Herrera is a California Chicano who teaches creative writing at the University of California at Riverside. Herrera also writes children's books, songs and fiction. *Cinnamon Girl* and *Downtown Boy* are his most recent young adult novels.

Carl Sandburg

CAROLYN FORCHÉ (1950-)
9. **"The Colonel"**
Originally collected in *The Country Between Us*, 1981
Recorded at the Folger Shakespeare Library, Washington, D.C., 1981
From the album *Ourselves Or Nothing*, Watershed Foundation #WTC-137, 1982

Carolyn Forché is a poet, translator and editor of the 1993 anthology *Against Forgetting: Twentieth Century Poetry Of Witness*. She has received the Yale Series of Younger Poets Award, the Lamont Award of the Academy of American Poets, the *Los Angeles Times* Book Award and, most recently, her book *Blue Hour* was a finalist for the National Book Critics Circle Award. She teaches at Skidmore College in Saratoga Springs, New York.

PETER BALAKIAN (1951-)
10. **"The History Of Armenia"**
Originally collected in *Sad Days Of Light*, 1983
Recorded by Rebekah Presson Mosby, January 2001

Balakian's memoir, *Black Dog Of Fate* (1997), named a *New York Times* Notable Book of the Year, recalls the Armenian genocide of 1915 through the author's family's experiences. His most recent book of poems is *June Tree: New And Selected Poems 1974-2000*. Balakian is a professor of English at Colgate University.

JOY HARJO (1951-)
11. **"Grace"**
Originally collected in *In Mad Love And War*, 1990
From the album *Native Joy For Real*, Mekko Records, 2004

Joy Harjo is an enrolled member of the Muskogee Indian Tribe and a jazz saxophonist whose band is called Joy Harjo and Poetic Justice. In 1991 she received the American Book Award from the Before Columbus Foundation and the Poetry Society of America's William Carlos Williams Award for her book of poems *In Mad Love And War*. She teaches at UCLA.

RITA DOVE (1952-)
12. **"Parsley"**
Originally collected in *Museum*, 1983
Recorded in San Diego, CA, for *New Letters On The Air*, 1985

Rita Dove won the Pulitzer Prize for her book *Thomas And Beulah* (1986), which was based on the lives of her African American grandparents, who lived in Ohio. Dove has served as Poet Laureate of the United States and of the Commonwealth of Virginia. She teaches at the University of Virginia, sings opera, plays classical music and dances the tango.

VIJAY SESHADRI (1954-)
13. "The Long Meadow"
Originally collected in *The Long Meadow*, 2004
Recorded by Rebekah Presson Mosby in New York City, July 28, 2005

Born in India, Seshadri grew up in Ohio. A former editor and writer for *The New Yorker*, Seshadri now directs the Graduate Program in Creative Nonfiction at Sarah Lawrence College and lives in Brooklyn. His book *The Long Meadow* (2004) won the James Laughlin Award from the Academy of American Poets.

MARILYN CHIN (1955-)
14. "The Floral Apron"
Originally collected in *The Phoenix Gone, The Terrace Empty*, 1994
From a broadcast on NPR's *All Things Considered*, May 26, 1999

Marilyn Chin was born in Hong Kong and raised in Portland, Oregon. Her latest book is *Rhapsody In Plain Yellow* (2002). She also translated a book of poems by the contemporary Chinese poet Ai Qing. She codirects the MFA program at San Diego State University.

LUCI TAPAHONSO (1953-)
15. "Raisin Eyes"
Originally collected in *A Breeze Swept Through*, 1987
Recorded in Kansas City, MO, for *New Letters On The Air*, 1992

Luci Tapahonso was raised on the Navajo reservation in Shiprock, Arizona, where she spoke first Diné (Navajo) and then English. To date, her work sometimes incorporates bits of Diné language. Tapahonso is a professor of English at the University of Arizona, Tucson. Her most recent book of poems is *Blue Horses Rush In* (1997).

LUIS RODRIGUEZ (1954-)
16. "The Concrete River"
Originally collected in *The Concrete River*, 1991
Recorded in Kansas City, MO, for *New Letters On The Air*, 1992

Rodriguez's early poems often recall his youth in Los Angeles gangs, also the subject of his best-selling memoir, which was a *New York Times* Notable Book of the Year, *Always Running: La Vida Loca, Gang Days In L.A.* (1993). His latest poetry title is *My Nature Is Hunger: New & Selected Poems 1989-2004*.

Adrienne Rich

LI-YOUNG LEE (1957-)

17. **"My Father, In Heaven, Is Reading Out Loud"**
Originally collected in *The City In Which I Love You*, 1990
Recorded in Chicago for *New Letters On The Air*, 1990

Li-Young Lee's father was Chinese and the personal physician to Mao Zedong. Lee was born in Indonesia and fled with his family to many Asian countries before coming to America in 1964. *Book Of My Nights* (2001) is Lee's most recent book of poems. He lives in Chicago.

ELISE PASCHEN (1959-)

18. **"Two Standards"**
Originally collected in *Infidelities*, Story Line Press, 1996
Recorded at WBEZ, Chicago, Illinois

Elise Paschen is a former director of the Poetry Society of America who helped found the Poetry in Motion project on New York's subways and buses. She is the daughter of ballerina Maria Tallchief, an Osage Indian. Paschen's latest book of poems is *Infidelities* (1996). She teaches at the Art Institute of Chicago.

DEBORAH GARRISON (1961-)

19. **"I Saw You Walking"**
Originally published in *The New Yorker*
Recorded by Rebekah Presson Mosby in New York City, July 28, 2005

A former editor at *The New Yorker*, Deborah Garrison is now poetry editor for Knopf. Her latest book of poems is *A Working Girl Can't Win* (1998).

ELIZABETH ALEXANDER (1962-)

20. **"The female seer will burn upon this pyre"**
21. **"After The Gig: Mick Jagger"**
Originally collected in *Antebellum Dream Book*, 2001
Recorded by Rebekah Presson Mosby in New York City, July 29, 2005

Elizabeth Alexander is the author of four books of poetry, the most recent of which is *American Sublime* (2005). Alexander often explores her African American heritage through persona and historical poems. She teaches at Yale University.

D.A. POWELL (1963-)

22. **"[morning broke on my cabin inverted, tempest in my forehead]"**
Originally collected in *Cocktails*, 2004
Recorded on August 25, 2005, at KQED, San Francisco

Powell is the author of three books of poems that often refer to his experiences as a gay man, the most recent of which is *Cocktails* (2004). He teaches at the University of San Francisco.

E.E. Cummings

Ezra Pound

CARL HANCOCK RUX (1964-)
23. **"Eleven More Days"**
From the album *Apothecary Rx*
Giant Step Records #GSTEP 7040-2

Rux is a poet, singer, songwriter and actor whose poetic opera will be performed at the Brooklyn Academy of Music in 2006. His debut collection of poems and prose, *Pagan Operetta*, came out in 2000. Rux's work tends to mix popular culture, hip-hop and an interest in classical literature.

JOHN POCH (1966-)
24. **"Simon Peter"**
Unpublished
Recorded live at Colgate University, March 4, 2004

John Poch is the editor of *32 Poems* magazine and teaches at Texas Tech University in Lubbock. His most recent book is *Ghost Towns Of The Enchanted Circle* (2006).

SUJI KWOCK KIM (1968-)
25. **"Fragments Of The Forgotten War"**
Collected in *Notes From The Divided Country* (Academy of American Poets, 2003)
Recorded by Rebekah Presson Mosby at WAMC, Albany, August 2, 2005

Kim teaches at Sarah Lawrence College. Her book of poems, whose title refers to Korea, is *Notes From The Divided Country* (2003).

KEVIN PRUFER (1969-)
26. **"Lucky Criminals"**
Originally collected in *The Finger Bone* (Carnegie Mellon University Press, 2002)
Recorded in Kansas City, 2004

Kevin Prufer has published three books of poems, most recently, *Fallen From A Chariot* (2005). Prufer teaches at Central Missouri State University.

KEVIN YOUNG (1970-)
27. **"The Slaughter"**
Originally collected in *Most Way Home*, 1995
Recorded in Kansas City, MO, for *New Letters On The Air*, 1995

Kevin Young's first book, *Most Way Home* (1995), was selected for the National Poetry Series. Young's poetic interests include art, especially that of Jean-Michel Basquiat, and jazz. Young teaches at Emory University. His most recent book of poems is *Black Maria* (2005).

JONATHAN LAMFERS (1981-)
28. **"scab"**
Unpublished
Recorded at WFPL in Louisville, Kentucky, August 24, 2005

Jonathan Lamfers is a recent graduate of Colgate University. He lives in Louisvillle, Kentucky.

NOTE: Unless otherwise qualified, the term *Poet Laureate* refers here to the position of Poet Laureate of the United States, which was, until 1991, known as Poetry Consultant to the Library of Congress.

In the case of most of the poets featured on the first three CDs, there is a book of selected and/or collected poems which can be obtained by those with an interest in pursuing an author's work further.

DISC ONE

"**Lucinda Matlock**" courtesy of Hilary Masters; "**The Creation**" courtesy of The American Speech Collection, Rare Book and Manuscript Library, Columbia University; "**If I Told Him: A Completed Portrait Of Picasso**," "**Helen In Egypt (excerpt)**," "**Résumé**" and "**The Lady's Reward**" courtesy of Arthur Luce Klein & Associates; "**So And So Reclining On Her Couch**" used by permission of Alfred A. Knopf, a division of Random House, Inc., © 92nd Street Y, 2006; ℗ 92nd Street Y, 2006; "**The Red Wheelbarrow**," "**To Elsie**" and "**Hugh Selwyn Mauberly**" courtesy of New Directions Publishing Corp.; "**Journey Of The Magi**" © The TS Eliot Estate, courtesy of Faber and Faber; "**Recuerdo**" and "**Love Is Not All**" courtesy of The Edna St. Vincent Millay Society; "**as freedom is a breakfastfood**" copyright 1940, © 1968, 1991 by the Trustees for the E.E. Cummings Trust, from *Complete Poems: 1904-1962* by E.E. Cummings, edited by George J. Firmage, used by permission of Liveright Publishing Corporation; "**To Juan At The Winter Solstice**" and "**The Cave Of Nakedness**" courtesy of American Academy Of Poets; "**John Brown's Body**" copyright © 1927, 1928 by Stephen Vincent Benet, copyright renewed © 1955 by Rosemary Carr Benet, used by permission of Brandt & Hochman Literary Agents, Inc.; "**Strong Men**" courtesy of John L. Dennis, Literary Executor for Sterling Brown; "**The Negro Speaks Of Rivers**" and "**The Weary Blues**" courtesy of Harold Ober & Associates; "**Portrait Of The Artist As A Prematurely Old Man**" used by permission of Curtis Brown Ltd., copyright © 1934 by Ogden Nash. All Rights Reversed; "**King Of The River**" courtesy of Darhansoff & Verrill Literary Agency; "**I Knew A Woman**" and "**Elegy For Jane**" courtesy of Smithsonian Folkways Recordings; "**Late Air**" and "**The Fish**" from *The Complete Poems 1927-1979* by Elizabeth Bishop, copyright © 1979, 1983 by Alice Helen Methfessel.

DISC TWO

"**Those Winter Sundays**" courtesy of Copper Canyon Press; "**The Ballad Of Orange And Grape**" and "**To Be A Jew In The Twentieth Century**" courtesy of International Creative Management, as agents for Muriel Rukeyser; **#23 ("The Lay Of Ike")** and **#36 ("The high ones die…")** copyright © 1969 by John Berryman, copyright renewed 1992 by Kate Donahue Berryman, audio courtesy of American Academy Of Poets; "**The world is so difficult to give up…**," "**This is the solution to be happy with slaughter…**," "**Here I am with mike in hand, shooting down the rapids…**," "**I killed a fly…**" and "**What about dying?…**" © 1991 by David Ignatow and reused by permission of Wesleyan University Press; "**Passing Remark**" and "**Serving With Gideon**" from *The Way It Is*, Graywolf Press, 1998, courtesy of The Estate of William Stafford and Graywolf Press; "**And Death Shall Have No Dominion**" and "**The Tombstone Told When She Died**" courtesy of Harold Ober Associates Inc.; "**The Mother**" and "**We Real Cool**" courtesy of Brooks Permissions; "**Skunk Hour**" from *Collected Poems* by Robert Lowell, copyright © 2003 by Harriett Lowell and Sheridan Lowell; "**Crossing Over**" courtesy of William Meredith; "**See it was like this when…**" and "**Underwear**" courtesy of The Watershed Foundation; "**The Secret Of My Endurance**" courtesy of Denny Bruce; "**Ray**" courtesy of Copper Canyon Press; "**Love Calls Us To The Things Of This World**" courtesy of Richard Wilbur; "**American Haikus**" produced under license from Rhino Entertainment Company, a Warner Music Group company; "**Death Psalm: O Lord Of Mysteries**" courtesy of New Directions Publishing Corp., audio courtesy of Woodberry Poetry Room, Houghton Library, Harvard College Library; "**Monet Refuses The Operation**" courtesy of Louisiana State University Press from *Alive Together: New And Selected Poems* by Lisel Mueller, copyright © 1996 Lisel Mueller; "**Woodchucks**" courtesy of Maxine Kumin; "**America**" courtesy of the Allen Ginsberg Trust; "**Still**" courtesy of Phyllis Ammons; used by permission of Alfred A. Knopf, a division of Random House, Inc., © 92nd Street Y, 2006; ℗ 92nd Street Y, 2006; "**My Philosophy Of Life**" courtesy of American Academy Of Poets; "**After Making Love We Hear Footsteps**" and "**Last Gods**" courtesy of Galway Kinnell; "**A Blessing**" from *The Branch Will Not Break* © 1963 by James Wright and by permission of Wesleyan University Press; "**All My Pretty Ones**" and "**For My Lover, Returning To His Wife**" used by permission of Sterling Lord Literistic, Inc., copyright by Anne Sexton.

DISC THREE

"**Even In Paris**" courtesy of Richard Howard; "**Diving Into The Wreck**," "**The Song Of The Taste**," "**Why I Take Good Care Of My Macintosh Computer**," "**The Idea Of Ancestry**," "**The Poem**" and "**Odysseus To Telemachus**" courtesy of The Watershed Foundation; "**Lovesong**" courtesy of Faber and Faber; "**Omeros (excerpt)**" from "Chapter LXIV" from *Omeros* by Derek Walcott, copyright © 1990 by Derek Walcott; "**Daddy**" courtesy of the Brady Literary Management, on behalf of the Estate of Jospeh P. Berk; "**The Greatest Poem In The World**" courtesy of David Ray; "**And Oddly Lovely Day Alone**" courtesy of John Updike; "**Bang, Bang Outishly**," "**Rhythim Blues**" and "**Shazam Doowah**" used by permission of Sterling Lord Literistic, Inc; "**Dahomey**" courtesy of The Charlotte Sheedy Literary Agency, Inc.; "**Right To Life**" copyright © 1973, 1982 by Marge Piercy/Middlemarsh, Inc., from *Louder: We Can't Hear You (Yet!)*, Leapfrog Press, 2004; "**Zimmer Imagines Heaven**" courtesy of Paul Zimmer; "*cruelty. don't talk to me about cruelty*" courtesy of BOA Editions, Ltd.; "**I Have Had To Learn To Live With My Face**" courtesy of Diane Wakoski; "**We were so poor…**" "**I was stolen by the gypsies…**" and "**Everybody knows the story**" courtesy of Charles Simic; "**Death Of A Naturalist**" from *Opened Ground: Selected Poems 1966-1996* by Seamus Heaney, copyright © 1998 by Seamus Heaney, audio courtesy of Woodberry Poetry Room, Houghton Library, Harvard College Library; "**Lester Leaps In**" and "**A Dance For Militant Dilettantes**" courtesy of Al Young; "**Fire**" courtesy of Gloria Vando; "**Sometimes It's Better To Laugh 'Honest Injun'**" Courtesy of Simon J. Ortiz; "**Ode To My Shoes**" courtesy of Erica Jong.

DISC FOUR

"**Wonder**" courtesy of Sharon Olds; "**The Lost Pilot**" courtesy of James Tate; "**Puerto Rican Obituary**" courtesy of Smithsonian Folkways Recordings; "**Uh Oh Plutonium**" courtesy of Anne Waldman; "**The Fine Printing On The Label Of A Bottle Of Non-Alcoholic Beer**" and "**The Sweat Lodge**" courtesy of Adrian Louis; "**Facing It**" recorded and reprinted by permission of Wesleyan University Press; "**Logan Heights And The World**" courtesy of Juan-Felipe Herrera; "**The Colonel**" courtesy of Carolyn Forché; "**The History Of Armernia**" courtesy of Peter Balakian; "**Grace**" courtesy of Joy Harjo; "**Parsley**" courtesy of Rita Dove; "**The Long Meadow**" © 2004 by Vijay Seshadri, used with the permission of Graywolf Press, Saint Paul, Minnesota; "**The Floral Apron**" from *The Phoenix Gone, The Terrace Empty* (Minneapolis: Milkweed Editions, 1994), copyright © 1994 by Marilyn Chin, reused with permission from Milkweed Editions; "**Raisin Eyes**" courtesy of Luci Tapahonso; "**The Concrete River**" courtesy of Luis Rodriguez; "**My Father, In Heaven, Is Reading Out Loud**" courtesy of Li-Young Lee; "**Two Standards**" courtesy of Elise Paschen; "**I Saw You Walking**" from *The Second Child* by Deborah Garrison, copyright © 2006 by Deborah Garrison, used by permission of Random House, Inc.; "**The female seer will burn upon this pyre**" and "**After The Gig: Mick Jagger**" courtesy of The Faith Childs Literary Agency; "**[morning broke on my cabin inverted, tempest in my forehead]**" courtesy of D.A. Powell; "**Eleven More Days**" courtesy of Giant Step Records Inc. / Music Art Management, Inc. 2004, www.gianstep.net; "**Simon Peter**" courtesy of John Poch; "**Fragments Of The Forgotten War**" courtesy of Suki Kwock Kim (www.sujikwockkim.com); "**Lucky Criminals**" from the book *Fallen From A Chariot* (Carnegie Mellon 2005), courtesy of Carnegie Mellon University Press; "**The Slaughter**" courtesy of Kevin Young; "**scab**" courtesy of Jonathan Lamfers.

**Compiled & Produced by
Rebekah Presson Mosby**

Project Supervision: **Derek Dressler and Julee Stover**
Licensing: **Rebekah Presson Mosby**
Business Affairs: **Dave McIntosh**
Remastering: **Randy Perry at Basement Tapes**
Tape Transfer Engineer for Library of Congress
    Material: **Larry Appelbaum**
Art Direction, Design and Typographic
    Illustrations: **Intersection Studio**
Artwork/Package Supervision: **Jeff Palo**
Photography: **© Bettmann/CORBIS**
Project Assistance: **John Roberts and Emily Johnson**

 D4K 10029

℗ & © 2006 Shout! Factory LLC, 2042-A Armacost Ave., Los Angeles,
CA 90025. All Rights Reserved./Distributed by Sony BMG Music
Entertainment Inc./550 Madison Avenue, New York, NY 10022-3211.